ULTIMATE

DRAMA ACTIVITIES FOR THE CLASSROOM

BY JOANNE WATKINSON

Salamander Street

First published in 2021 by Salamander Street Ltd.
(info@salamanderstreet.com)

Ultimate Drama Activities for the Classroom © Joanne Watkinson, 2021

9781914228131

10 9 8 7 6 5 4 3 2 1

Joanne Watkinson is a writer from Yorkshire. She started writing when she was a teenager, and continued to do so through to adulthood, although it took nearly two decades before she allowed anyone to read anything she'd written. In the early nineties Joanne studied Performing Arts in Cheltenham, Gloucestershire gaining a BA Hons, and went on to study for a PGCE in Drama and English at Bretton Hall college. In 1996 she took up a Drama and English teaching post at a school in South Yorkshire where she stayed for nineteen years heading up a successful performing arts department. Alongside her teaching commitments she examined for GCSE and A-Level practical exams travelling around the country. After a devastating set back due to a serious illness, she made the difficult decision to leave her teaching career to fulfil a dream of opening her own theatre school and becoming a writer.

Elite Theatre Arts opened in Doncaster nearly six years ago and continues to go from strength to strength. Last year Joanne set herself a new challenge and started up ETA Management, a casting agency for children and young adults, she continued writing alongside setting up the businesses and after several successful years of self-publishing, her monologues were picked up by LAMDA for their recent Anthology. Working with children has always been an important part of Joanne's career and to date she has directed over fifty plays and shows across Yorkshire including some of her own material, which she continues to enjoy writing. Joanne is so pleased to have joined forces with Salamander Street, and is looking forward to new goals and opportunities.

Contents

WARM UP GAMES

IMPROVISATION AND DEVISING

IMPROVISATION FOR LARGE GROUPS

WORKING WITH SCRIPT

WARM UP GAMES

Some traditional games, and others with a modern take, as well as a basic improvisation scenario following each game.

Name Game

Performers stand in a circle and swap places by saying their own name and the name of the person whose place they intend to take.

Improv: Choose a scenario where roles are reversed (characters swap places). For example, a child who is acting like the parent. This could lead into a lesson about stage status.

Name and Gesture

A good introduction game is for performers to perform a gesture to introduce themselves along with their name. In turns, everyone repeats. You can then play the above name game using gestures only.

Improv: Improvise a scene where only gesture is allowed in order to tell the story.

Introduction Game

In turns, performers introduce themselves and tell the group something they like. the thing they like must begin with the first letter of their name. You can then play the above Name Game using the thing they like instead of names.

Improv: Create a scenario where two characters meet for the first time.

Wink Murder

Performers stand in a circle, one murderer (without the knowledge of the detective) and one detective are chosen. The murderer winks to 'kill' their victims. The detective has three guesses to figure out who the murderer is. A variation could be having the performers move around the circle.

Improv: In groups, create a murder mystery scene.

The teacher tapes around the outline of a body on the floor and props (clues) are placed around it in the space. The scenes could include:

a. Interviews with suspects.

b. News reports.

c. Re-enactment for TV.

d. A flashback to show what really happened.

e. The court hearing.

This could develop into a devised piece of theatre.

Who's Changing the Movement?

Same rules as Wink Murder but instead of winking, the suspect tries to change the movement of the group by having the other performers copy them. The detective has three guesses to figure out who the suspect is.

Improv: Improvise a scene using a starting line from this book. One of the performers must try to change the direction of the scene. If successful, the scene should change and end as something different to how it started. The teacher should tell the performer from each group the objective in secret.

Blood Potato

One or two performers are chosen to be the 'blood potato'. Everyone walks around the room slowly. If contact is made with another performer, they whisper potato to each other. If contact is made with the blood potato, they must whisper 'blood potato', and the performer is out.

Improv: There is a dangerous person among us, perhaps a traitor. In groups, create a scene where one character is causing conflict.

Do This

One person leads the class in a physical warm up. Before each move they say, 'Do this.' However, if they say, 'Do that' before a movement then those performers which copied that move are out. For a further challenge, ask performers to balance a foam square on their heads. If it falls off, they are out.

Improv: Improvise a scene where one character has the power to make the other characters do things they wouldn't ordinarily do.

Ladders

In pairs, the performers sit foot-to-foot creating a ladder across the room. Each pair is given an animal. The teacher or chosen performer tells a story which includes the named animals. Whenever a pair hears their animal, they race down the ladder (over people's feet), then around the outside of the ladder and back to their seats. The winner is the first one back in their seated position. Other possible themes could be Christmas objects, characters from a fairy tale, film titles etc.

Improv: Use the characters from this game to develop a scene. It could lead into a session based around the following Christmas themed script:

Night of the Reindeer

DANCER: Will you slow down, Dasher, you're going to cause an accident.

DASHER: We need to get around the whole world in one night, there's every reason to dash.

VIXEN: Dasher, don't listen to Dancer. Dasher by name, dashing by nature.

BLITZEN: I think you've actually made him blush.

CUPID: Do I detect love in the air?

DASHER: Cupid!

CUPID: I'm named after the Roman god of love for a reason.

VIXEN: I don't need any help from you, Cupid. I know how to impress the stags.

DONNER: Sure you do. Rudolf, you're quiet tonight.

RUDOLF: Just doing my job, Donner, guiding the way. Comet, what's your forecast on the night skies this Christmas Eve?

COMET: Pretty clear for most of the world, we may even get to see the northern lights over Iceland.

CUPID: How romantic eh, Dasher.

PRANCER: Stop teasing him, Cupid.

CUPID: You just keep the timing, Prancer.

PRANCER: Everything in counts of eight eh, Dancer.

DANCER: Absolutely, Prancer, we need perfect timing. I could have been on *Dancing with the Stars*, you know.

PRANCER: Sure you could've.

VIXEN: I'd like to dance with you.

CUPID: You'd dance with any deer.

VIXEN: Watch your mouth, Cupid, you're just jealous of my good looks and stunning antlers.

COMET: Ladies, please. Just enjoy the night sky. Look, a shooting star!

RUDOLF: Beautiful.

DANCER: Sure is, Rudolf. Like dancing stars.

RUDOLF: Dancing stars.

BLITZEN: Hey guys, I don't mean to panic anyone, but aren't we missing something? Or should I say someone?

DONNER: Roll call. (*They all respond with 'present' after each name.*) Dasher? Dancer? Prancer? Comet? Cupid? Me? Blitzen? Rudolf?

DASHER: Hey what about, Vix?

VIXEN: Yeah guys, what about me?

DONER: Doh! (*Meaning doe.*)

VIXEN: Oh, ha ha!

RUDOLF: I don't get it.

BLITZEN: He's got no I*deer*! (*Laughs.*)

VIXEN: Doe, doe, a deer…a female deer!

RUDOLF: Oh.

COMET: How long have you been waiting to crack that one, Donner?

DASHER: So, we are all present and correct.

VIXEN: Present!

RUDOLF: Present…present…presents! We have no presents!!

BLITZEN: And that's because...anyone? We are missing...anyone... anyone?

ALL: Santa!

DANCER: We left Santa!

ALL: Oh deer!

Questions

Performers sit in a circle on chairs/mats. The teacher asks yes/no questions. If the answer is yes, the performer must find a new chair/ mat. Each time one chair/mat is taken away and that person is out.

Suggested questions:

Do you have a pet dog?
Were you in a play last year?
Are you wearing something blue?
Do you have siblings?
Do you like school?
Do you have a birthday in July?

Improv: Spontaneous improvisation with one rule; you may only ask questions.

Keeper of the Keys

Performers sit in a circle. The performer who is 'on' sits on a chair in the centre, blindfolded. Keys are placed under the chair which the performer at the centre must guard. In turn, performers try to steal the keys without the guard tapping them. When someone manages to take them without being caught, they become the guard.

Improv: A fantasy theme set in a castle where something important is being protected.

What Are You Doing?

Performers stand in a circle. The first performer enters the circle and starts a mime, e.g. making breakfast. The second performer says, 'What are you doing?' They reply with something other than what they are actually doing, for example, ballet dancing. The second performer must take on this mime until they are asked what they are doing and so on. The teacher decides when to end the game.

Improv: In pairs use your mimes from the game and develop into a scene.

Stage Directions

This is a great game to get the performers familiar with the areas of a stage.

UP STAGE RIGHT	UP STAGE CENTRE	UP STAGE LEFT
CENTRE STAGE RIGHT	CENTRE STAGE	CENTRE STAGE LEFT
DOWN STAGE RIGHT	DOWN STAGE CENTRE	DOWN STAGE LEFT

The performers gather centre stage. The teacher calls out an area on the stage and the last performer to move to that area is out.

Here are some added rules that the teacher can call out:

Shakespeare – The performers say 'To be or not to be that is the question.'

Panto – The performers say 'He's behind you.'

Paint the scenery – The performers go down to the floor and mime painting.

End of the show – The performers bow or curtsey.

Steal the limelight – They do something to catch the teacher's attention.

Finally, when 'double act' is called everyone must link arms with a partner. Anyone left is out.

For a Christmas themed variation to this game, you can use the below stage directions:

Santa's Coming – Performers shout 'Ho, Ho, Ho' while rubbing their bellies.

Elves at work – Performers kneel and mime wrapping presents.

Christmas morning – Performers act overexcited.

Snow is falling – Performers say 'Brrr' while hugging body.

Do you want to build a snowman? – Performers mime building a snowman with a partner (if you don't find a partner you're out).

Starry night – Jazz hands.

Christmas Eve – Performers pretend to be asleep.

Jingle Bells – Performers shake hands from top to bottom singing Jingle Bells.

Queen's speech – Performers curtsey or bow.

Snowball fight – Performers mime a snowball fight.

Improv: Take one of the starting lines from this book and create a scene where all areas on the stage are used. You could use one of the added rules as a theme or style, e.g. in the style of a pantomime or a scenario where someone is trying to steal the limelight.

Prisoner and Guard

Performers are divided into 'prisoners' and 'guards'. The prisoners are seated in chairs in a circle, with a guard standing behind them. One chair is left empty, the guard with the empty chair must try and steal a prisoner by nodding at someone in the circle. If nodded at, the prisoner must make a run for it. If their guard taps them on the shoulder the prisoner remains theirs. Once they get the hang of it, try it with a second empty chair. The teacher decides when to end the game.

Improv: Performers set their scene in a prison where a prisoner and a guard find some common ground. This could also lead into some scripted work using the scene *Chapped* where a homeless girl is caught shoplifting by the shop's security guard.

Chapped

SECURITY GUARD: Sit down.

MARY: Fine.

SECURITY GUARD: You took a lipstick without paying, young lady, what do you expect?

MARY: It wasn't a lipstick; it was just a lip balm.

SECURITY GUARD: That's irrelevant.

MARY: Ok I know it's wrong. But my lips are, you know, all cracked. It's cold out there.

SECURITY GUARD: Are you trying to pull the sympathy card?

MARY: I'm not trying to get your sympathy, people like you don't feel anything.

SECURITY GUARD: Really?

MARY: Every case is the same to you, doesn't really matter why I took the lip balm. Let's face it, if I wanted to make my fortune, I wouldn't have taken moisturiser for lips now would I?

SECURITY GUARD: Quit giving me lip.

MARY: No pun intended.

SECURITY GUARD: You're giving me cheek.

MARY: I'm not being cheeky, just factual. Look, it's just real cold this time of year and my lips get sore.

SECURITY GUARD: Why don't you just ask your parents for some money for lip balm? Don't you kids get pocket money these days?

MARY: You think that's the answer? Well I can't, Sherlock.

SECURITY GUARD: I told you to watch your lip.

MARY: I can't go home.

SECURITY GUARD: Why?

MARY: I just can't ok.

SECURITY GUARD: Don't get testy.

MARY: I'm not getting testy. I just can't go home.

SECURITY GUARD: Well, I'm going to need to call your parents.

MARY: Listen, Mr Hot Shot Security Guard, I can't go home because I don't have a home to go to. You'd never make a detective.

SECURITY GUARD: You need to button it with the insults.

MARY: Ok sorry, that was a bit cheeky. But come on, dude look at me. Don't you recognise me at all?

SECURITY GUARD: Should I?

MARY: You walk past me every day on the way to this poxy job. Annoyingly, you're always whistling the Star Wars theme tune, while you stuff your face with a doughnut and wash it down with a chocolate smoothie. You pass me at the same time every day and every day you avert your eyes so that you don't have to acknowledge me.

SECURITY GUARD: I haven't averted my eyes or avoided eye contact, maybe I was just going about my business.

MARY: Don't worry I get it. It's awkward to look someone in the eye that you don't want to help, that you have no respect for, that you consider a complete waste of space. I know you think people like me dirty your streets, that we are all bad to the core. That if we beg for money, it's for drugs not food. Hey look, go ahead arrest me.

SECURITY GUARD: I'm not going to arrest you. Not this time anyway.

MARY: Please do. Do you know why I'm really here, sat before you having this moment of shame?

SECURITY GUARD: Because you have chapped lips?

MARY: It's because I chose to be. You're right about one thing, it didn't really matter whether I took a balm stick, lipstick or flaming chopstick! It wasn't about what I took, it was about why I took it.

SECURITY GUARD: Enlighten me.

MARY: It's cold out there, my lips *are* chapped, I'm tired and I want one night of shelter. Just one.

SECURITY GUARD: And you thought stealing would accomplish that?

MARY: Look just go ahead, do your job and arrest me. Lock me up for the night. Please.

SECURITY GUARD: That's why you took a lipstick?

MARY: Lip balm! Never mind. That's what I came for, I let you catch me. I can shoplift without getting caught, you know. It's not that hard.

SECURITY GUARD: I'm going to have to contact your parents.

MARY: Good luck with that.

SECURITY GUARD: Or social services.

MARY: No, don't. Look we can both win here; I get a night in the security of a cell and you get brownie points for catching me. But next time you walk past me remember that the girl with the chapped lips just wanted eye contact, acknowledgement of her existence and one night of shelter.

Knots

Performers stand in a circle and reach across with their right hand for another performer's hand, then the same with their left. They have to unravel themselves without letting go of any hands, until they form a circle or two interlocking circles.

If you have enough performers, it's good to have teams and challenge them to be the first to finish.

Improv: The theme is 'sticking together,' however, if during the game your circle was broken then your improv must show a moment of broken trust.

What Time Is It Mr/Mrs Wolf?

A performer is chosen to be Mr/Mrs Wolf. The rest of the performers stand at the opposite end of the space. Mr/Mrs Wolf has their back to everyone. The performers, in turn say:

'What time is it Mr/Mrs Wolf?'

The wolf replies with a time e.g. two o'clock and that performer takes two steps forward, and so on. If the wolf replies 'Dinner time', all performers run back to where they started, trying not to be caught by the wolf. The aim is to get to the other side without getting caught.

Improv: Take the story of the three little pigs and create one of the following:

     a. A news report

     b. A court scene

     c. A therapy session

The scenario should turn the story on its head, with the wolf turning out to be the victim or having valid reasons for his behaviour.

Stuck in the Mud

One performer is chosen to be 'on' and tries to catch the other performers. If caught, the performer stands with legs apart and arms outstretched until another performer frees them by crawling between their legs or running under their arms. A variation could be that when a performer is caught, they are given a theme by the person who is 'on', and they must talk continuously about that theme until freed.

Some themes could be:

- Christmas
- Newspapers
- School
- Climate change
- The government
- Exercise
- Acting
- Celebrity status
- Furniture
- Friends

Improv: Performers turn one of their themed talks into a monologue, or group work could be to polish an improvisation in the style of a news report which incorporates each performers' given theme.

Themed Human Bingo

Two or more large grids (4x4 squares) are placed on the floor and performers are divided into two or more teams. The grids have answers to questions on them and each grid differs. They could be themed, for example they could all be answers to questions about musicals, plays, music, drama vocabulary, or perhaps Christmas themed depending on the time of year.

The teacher asks a question and if a performer knows the answer they jump onto that square of the grid. When four performers are stood on the grid in either a diagonal, horizontal or vertical line, or standing at each of the four corners of the grid, they shout 'Bingo.' If a performer gets a question wrong, they must step off of the grid and the game continues.

This can be played with younger students by changing the written answers to pictures.

Improv: Use one of the answers from the grid as the basis for a group improvisation.

Truth and Lie

Each performer tells the class one true story about themselves and one lie. The performers decide which is true and which is the lie. This can be made into a more physical warm up by asking each performer to tell just one of their stories whilst everyone else either runs stage right for true or stage left for false, those that get it wrong are out.

Improv: In groups choose one of the lies told in the game and use it as the basis for an improvisation. Perform the improv and then the audience gets to suggest ways to exaggerate the lie further and consequently the improv is reworked. This can be done more than once until the audience is happy with the outcome.

Mirrors

Start in a pair, one is the leader and one the follower. Subtle and slow controlled movements are created by the leader which the follower must mirror. The teacher tries to work out who is leading. The performers can then create groups of four, then eight, or work as a whole class with the teacher or chosen performer trying to detect who is leading. This activity can be done either in silence or with slow instrumental music, which can sometimes help the performers keep it controlled and avoid speeding the movement up.

Improv: The performers are given a scenario whereby a character can enter a mirror and meet their reflection. This game could also lead into a session where music is the stimulus. Performers would spend five minutes listening to the track and writing down whatever is in their head, this could be in narrative form, or simply the thoughts it provokes. The writing is then used as a basis for a polished improvisation, either solo or groups work.

Finger Snap

This is a simple game which can be played in pairs or as a whole class. The teacher simply counts to three, and on three everyone holds up however many fingers they choose. If the pairs hold up the same number of fingers, they shout 'Snap.' The winner is the first one to call 'Snap.' For the whole class version, the teacher would be at the front taking part and after counting to three, anyone with the same number of fingers as the teacher sits down and is out. This can also be played with gestures or poses.

Improv: In pairs, create an improvisation which has the theme of 'Snap.' Perhaps you attend the prom wearing exactly the same outfit as your friend, or you get exactly the same exam results as someone you've always been competitive with, or the improv could have a theme about twins.

The Rule Game

A performer is chosen to leave the room and a rule is given to the rest of the group. On the performer's return, they ask questions to members of the group, for example:

   a. What's your favourite colour?

   b. Who is your favourite band?

   c. What's your favourite subject at school?

   d. What did you do yesterday?

The members of the group must answer using the rule, while the chosen performer tries to work out what the rule is.

Examples of rules:

   a. Touch your hair when answering.

   b. Answer using the first letter of your name.

   c. Say 'erm' before you answer.

   d. Lie.

   e. Your answer must relate to a song title.

   f. Your answer must have only one syllable.

   g. You must change positions during your answer.

   h. Your answer must start with the last letter of the previous answer.

   i. Your answer must include one word from the question.

Improv: Create an improvisation where a code is cracked, or a rule is broken.

Emotions Exercise

Performer says 'I am unbelievably sad' but must show a different emotion, for example, frustration. Other performers can guess what emotion they're portraying. This can be developed further by passing the emotion to another performer.

E.g. Rebecca is depressed. Rebecca then says someone else's name and a different emotion but must say it in a depressed way as instructed by the previous performer.

Rebecca: Joe is depressed.

Joe: Emma is sad (delivered in a depressed way)

Emma: Tom is in love (delivered in a sad way)

And so on.

IMPROVISATION AND DEVISING

Drama Skills to Consider Before Performing

- Make sure the audience can see you (Don't perform with your back to them).
- Speak clearly and project so every word can be heard.
- Don't perform your entire piece up stage (At the back) move down stage (The front).
- Try to show your character physically, as well as vocally, and remember you are not playing yourself.
- Be controlled during any action (Don't run around the stage, you might be having a great time but the audience must know what's going on and therefore all movement requires purpose).
- Keep your focus, don't corpse (Don't giggle / come out of character).
- Perform with energy, this will make your audience enjoy it more.

Audience: Support everyone, clap at the end like it's the best thing you've ever seen!

What Is Improvisation?

- More often than not it is a spontaneous form of creating a scene, although it can be a starting point for a more polished performance. Improvisation is a fun way to explore new creations, it can generate ideas and create stimuli for further dramatic exploration.

In this section of the book you will find a number of starting points for improvisation work.

Improvisation rules to consider with your students:

- Create a safe and secure working environment.
- Don't pass judgement on other people's ideas.
- Don't block ideas, you will get more out of the scene if you go along with your partner's scenario.
- Avoid talking over another performer and trying to steal the scene. The scene needs to be controlled.
- Be encouraging.

Improvisation Exercises

Use the lines on pages 20-22 as starting points for the following improvisation exercises.

In pairs:

- Label the students A or B. A starts the improv using one of the starting lines. The pair continues until the teacher says freeze.
- As above, but A is only allowed to say two words at a time. This can be built upon, e.g. B can now only say two words at a time as well, this could develop into one line.
- B never lets A finish their lines; they must interrupt everything A tries to say.
- A and B must physically be at different levels at all times. E.g. If A chooses to sit during the improv and B is already seated, B must find a reason to stand or sit on the floor.
- The teacher says freeze during the improv. Either A or B is replaced with another performer who takes their physical position but must change the action so the scene moves into a different scenario.
- The last word A speaks in a line of dialogue must be the first line of B's next line and so on.
- Both performers must start each sentence with the first letter of their name.

- The teacher calls out 'pause' during the scene and the actors must only use facial expressions and gestures to continue the improv until the teacher calls 'dialogue.'

A third or fourth person can be added to the exercise to make it more challenging.

Starting Lines for Improvisation

1. Get down here and look at this.
2. Are you kidding me? It can't be stuck.
3. If I've told you once I have told you a thousand times.
4. It's not exactly difficult.
5. Take a step back and survey the situation.
6. You always act first, think later.
7. It has to be this way, I'm afraid.
8. You just need to knock and wait.
9. The big man will see you now.
10. Don't overreact, it's not like it hasn't happened before.
11. You need to stop panicking right now.
12. Where is everyone?
13. I don't like being alone.
14. Just count to ten.
15. Close your eyes and forget where you are.
16. Wow! This is exciting.
17. No, you can't have it.
18. I just want to experience it once.
19. You look terrified, try to fake it.
20. I like the word incredulous.
21. Open it slowly, you don't know what's inside.
22. I trusted you with a simple task.

23. Are you sure that's what you want?

24. If I could just squeeze past you.

25. I saw that first, it was in my trolley.

26. It's just a date, stop fretting.

27. Do I look nice in this?

28. I prefer what that girl is wearing.

29. I think I've won!

30. It only takes a few seconds.

31. Pass me that right now.

32. You have to be kidding me.

33. Jump in, it will be an adventure.

34. Did you really just say that out loud?

35. That's the best idea I've ever heard.

36. There's more space in here than you think.

37. I promise you'll be safe.

38. You open it, it's addressed to you.

39. Why did you let her speak to me like that?

40. If I say no that's what I mean.

41. You're doing it wrong.

42. You're a major disappointment.

43. Oh no! I've broken a nail.

44. Just use that hammer.

45. This is trespassing you know.

46. Why did you put on a big act in front of him?

47. I'm not asking you I'm telling you.

48. Stop pretending you're okay.

49. I asked you to keep it a secret.

50. It looks incredible, but what is it?

51. Are you telling me that the whole thing has been cancelled?

52. If you could just sit still for two minutes, I'll explain.

53. Please forgive me.

54. I am so excited! I can't believe you did all that for me.

55. And I said to him, "You can't tell anyone." So what does he do?!

56. I'm scared, I think we should go home.

57. You anger me!

58. You're going to have to speak up.

59. It's made of glass, please be careful.

60. Sometimes I feel like my life is one big performance.

Short Dialogue Extracts for Improvisation

These can work well for a more developed improvisation. You could give students a set time to prepare, or no time for a more spontaneous exercise. It can also be useful to set the amount of lines that can be added.

Students are encouraged to learn the dialogue, then extend the scene.

Buried

ONE: I've told you this is the spot.

TWO: Are you sure?

ONE: How many times?!!! Right here.

TWO: Pass me the spade.

ONE: Are you sure we should be doing this?

TWO: Look we have been having these conversations all week, just dig!

ONE: How can you even be so sure?

TWO: Dig!! Just dig!!

Are You Listening?

ONE: Are you listening to me?

TWO: Sure.

ONE: You're not.

TWO: I'm not?

ONE: No, you're not.

TWO: I'm not.

ONE: Is there something on your mind? I mean you're the one that invited me here.

TWO: I know I did.

ONE: You did.

TWO: I did.

ONE: Well, what's going on?

TWO: Well...

Breaking the News

ONE: I sat there by myself, just thinking. I was wondering how I would break the news when he/she arrived.

TWO: Hi, you said you needed to talk.

ONE: Hi, yes come and sit down.

TWO: *(Addressing the audience.)* She/he looked really nervous, my mind was spinning, why did she/he look so serious?

ONE: Can I get you a drink?

TWO: No thank you.

ONE: *(Addressing the audience.)* I didn't really want a drink either I was just stalling because I didn't know how to break the news...

I'm Home

ONE: I'm home. Did you hear me? I'm home.

TWO: Oh, hi.

ONE: Oh, hi? Is that it? Haven't you missed me?

TWO: You've only been gone ten minutes.

ONE: Have I?

TWO: Yes, you went out to get some custard creams.

ONE: Custard creams?

TWO: Yes, to have with our cup of tea.

ONE: Well, it felt like a lot longer because you'll never believe what happened when I was out...

Let Me Explain

ONE: Why are you looking at me like that?

TWO: I just can't believe what I'm hearing.

ONE: Do you need to sit down?

TWO: I think I need to lie down!

ONE: It's not that shocking...is it? Look, here's a chair.

TWO: Let me explain again...

Stuck

ONE: How long do you think we'll be stuck here?

TWO: Stop moaning.

ONE: I'm not moaning, I just want to get out of here.

TWO: I know we both do…

Baby

ONE: I really don't think we should be here.

TWO: It's fine no one is around.

ONE: Yes, but what if we get into trouble.

TWO: Stop being a baby.

ONE: I'm not being a baby; I just don't want my mum to ground me.

TWO: Your mum is at work so unless she has psychic powers she won't know.

For the following extracts, give the performers some planning time.

For development when creating a more polished improvisation, the performers could be taken through some of the following activities:

- Role on the wall
- Hot-seating
- Writing a monologue
- Thought tracking
- Thought tunnel
- Adding asides to give the audience insight into what they are really thinking

Looking Down

ONE: It's an incredible feeling to be so high up, look down there.

TWO: I can't!

For this scenario consider the following:

      a. Who are they?

      b. Where are they?

      c. Why are they there?

      d. Why can't the second character look down?

Open It

Two to three characters:

ONE: I didn't come here to cause trouble.

TWO: Why did you come?

ONE: I came to give you this (*They hand a box/letter over.*)

TWO/THREE: What is it?

ONE: Open it…

Continue…

Questions to consider:

- Who are the characters?
- Do you open it straight away? Which character actually opens it?
- What happened directly before this?
- What is in the box/letter?

Suggestions:

Box:

- Money
- A weapon
- A puppy
- Nothing

Letter:

- Eviction notice
- Death threat
- Inheritance
- A letter from a long lost relative/old friend
- A note from someone you thought wouldn't find you

Tips

To create tension, try to include dramatic pauses/moments of silence, where the audience has to read faces and body language.

Don't unravel the plot too quickly, make your audience think.

You could add a scene before this between Two and Three (if working in a group of three) to establish their characters.

Climax or Anti-Climax

Try using the extract below in two different ways. The first version should end dramatically, and the second on an anti-climax.

ONE: I saw you over there.

TWO: That's because I was over there.

ONE: Why didn't you just stay here?

TWO: Because I have nothing else to say to you.

ONE: Clearly you do, because you're here now.

TWO: Don't start with me.

ONE: Don't you speak to me like that.

TWO: Like what?

ONE: That! It wasn't my fault.

TWO: Well, whose fault was it?

ONE: It was just an accident.

TWO: Oh, is that what you call it?

ONE: Can't we just move on?

TWO: So you call _____ 'Just an accident'

Suggestions:

Scenario One

So you call <u>giving that girl your phone number</u> 'just an accident.'

Scenario Two

So you call <u>putting sugar in my coffee</u> 'just an accident.'

Performers could go on to improvise scenario two; or create a polished performance.

Performers could create a tension graph to demonstrate the high and low points in their performance, then evaluate the skills they used to achieve this.

For example:

- Facial expressions
- Gesture
- Posture
- Positioning
- Vocal expression/intonation
- Pitch and pause

- Vocal dynamics
- Stillness or movement
- Silence

Consider which character has the highest stage status and how this is demonstrated.

The following pages provide further scenarios for development through improvisation or devising.

Don't Be a Baby

ONE: Did you hear that?

TWO: I was trying to shut it out.

ONE: I heard it!

TWO: I don't like it here.

ONE: Why did you make us come here?

TWO: I told you, for the adventure.

ONE: Couldn't we have an adventure in a less scary location?

TWO: Don't be a baby.

ONE: If we get it on video, we will be rich.

TWO: How exactly?

ONE: Well the news would want it for a start.

TWO: No they wouldn't.

ONE: Why not?

TWO: Because they would say it's fake, everyone would.

ONE: They can tell these days if it's fake and I'm telling you I've seen it before and it's very real.

TWO: Now be brave and follow me. Shut the door behind you.

The Plan

ONE: Well I think that went to plan.

TWO: Really?

ONE: Yes, it seems to have worked.

TWO: Then why are we stuck in here?

ONE: Ah, well you see I only planned the first bit.

TWO: Right, so the crucial escape route bit you just thought we'd wing?

ONE: I didn't realise the building would go into lockdown when the alarm went off.

TWO: Ok, so you thought we would rob the place then just stroll out the front door? I only did this because you said it was fool proof! And I needed the money.

ONE: Just a small lapse in judgement. The next one will go better. We can plan it together.

TWO: Next one!? The only place we will be planning to escape from is prison!

ONE: Yeah well, that can be done too. I've seen it on the TV.

TWO: I give up, can't believe I didn't realise your level of stupidity before I pulled a pair of your mother's tights over my head. Did you get that idea from TV too?

ONE: Season one episode twenty-seven of CSI.

TWO: Think you need to start watching the Prison Break box set!

(Sirens can be heard.)

ONE: Too late!

Continue…

The Box

(Four children sit staring at a box they've found hidden in the woods.)

ONE: What do you think is in there?

TWO: I don't know.

THREE: I think it's a box of money.

FOUR: Then we should hand to the police.

THREE: We should spend it more like!

ONE: I think it's an ancient mystical object.

TWO: It might curse us!

ONE: Don't be ridiculous, you've read too many stories.

FOUR: I bet it's a magical game that transports you into different situations.

THREE: And brings animals from the jungle rampaging through your house!

ONE: You've watched Jumanji too many times!

TWO: What if it's a body?

ONE: Stop being so negative! Besides it's not big enough for a body.

TWO: A head?

THREE: Yep well done that's more positive! *(Sarcastically.)*

TWO: If you all thought it was something good you would have opened it already.

(The box moves.)

FOUR: Oh my days! Did you see that?

TWO: I can't look.

ONE: Open your eyes, that thing just moved.

THREE: Right one of us needs to open that thing.

ONE: I vote you!

THREE: Me? Why me?

ONE: You're the bravest!

THREE: Right, finders keepers, if its money it's mine!!

ONE, TWO AND THREE: Deal!!

(THREE opens the box.)

Continue…

Contrasting Scenes/Split Staging

Scene One

PARENT: What time do you call this?

KID: I'm only ten minutes late.

PARENT: Don't even try and give me the broken watch excuse, you're one hour late, I've been worried sick.

KID: Sorry, I lost track of time.

PARENT: You're always sorry. I bet you've been out with that new mate of yours again!

KID: So what?

PARENT: Don't speak to me like that. That group of so-called friends are bad news.

KID: Give me a break, will you? You would rather have me locked away in my room forever.

Scene Two

PARENT: Late again.

KID: Yeah, no big deal.

PARENT: To be honest I've been too busy watching the telly to notice.

KID: What's in to eat?

PARENT: You should've brought some chips with you.

KID: Got no money, have I?

PARENT: Don't start that again I'm skint, borrow some off your new mate, their family is loaded.

KID: Yeah whatever!

Using split staging continue to create these two scenes, remembering to freeze when the other pair is performing so that the audience knows where to focus their attention.

Contrasting Outcomes

ONE: I looked at you and I knew.

TWO: What?

ONE: I just knew straight away.

TWO: Straight away? What are you going on about?

ONE: I knew you weren't telling me everything.

TWO: Are you calling me a liar?

ONE: Your words not mine. I just need to know the whole story.

TWO: You seriously don't…

Continue…

Create two contrasting endings, e.g. one comical, one serious.

Short Scene Starters

Each scene starter could provide the beginning, middle or end of a polished improvisation.

Styles could also be explored. Perform the finished scene using one of the following genres:

a. Western

b. Musical

c. Action

d. Melodrama

e. Slapstick

f. Pantomime

g. Shakespearean

h. Horror

Extract One

ONE: Did you hear that?

TWO: I don't like the sound of that.

ONE: What do you think it is?

TWO: I'm scared.

ONE: I have a fantastic idea.

TWO: That's a first.

ONE: Hey, cheeky, I'm full of great ideas.

TWO: Okay, let's hear it.

Extract Two

ONE: You have a phone call.

TWO: Oh thanks. Hi, yes...yes...no...yes...ok bye.

ONE: Who was it?

TWO: You'll never believe it.

Extract Three

ONE: It wasn't my fault, I wasn't even there.

TWO: Of course, you weren't.

ONE: Really! I was nowhere to be seen.

TWO: So you're saying it happened all by itself?

ONE: If I could turn the clock back I would.

TWO: But you can't, so you might want to apologise.

ONE: I already said sorry!

TWO: I need more than that!

Extract Four

ONE: Tell me it's not true.

TWO: I can't.

ONE: How do I deal with this?

TWO: With my help.

Extract Five

ONE: What is that?

TWO: I don't know, I found it.

ONE: I think we should hand it in to the police.

TWO: I think it's finders keepers.

Extract Six

ONE: Stay calm.

TWO: I am calm.

ONE: You're not, you're shaking.

TWO: I'm trying to be calm, but would you be in my situation?

Extract Seven

ONE: Where are we?

TWO: I'm not sure. What happened?

ONE: I think we crashed.

TWO: I feel dizzy.

Extract Eight

ONE: Stay quiet. They will hear you.

TWO: Who will?

ONE: The zombies.

TWO: You're scaring me.

Alphabet Script

Performers create scenes using the alphabet as the first letter of each line. Here is an example.

ONE: Alex, how are you?

TWO: Better than I was, thank you.

ONE: Can you keep a secret?

TWO: Definitely! I love a good secret.

ONE: Excellent (*Whispers.*).

TWO: For goodness sake, Alex.

ONE: Great, isn't it?

TWO: Hardly!

ONE: If you can't be supportive then leave me alone.

ONE: Just think about it first.

TWO: Kick me when I'm down why don't you!

ONE: Let's just put this in perspective.

TWO: My perspective is perfectly in place!

ONE: Not really, if you're considering going ahead with this…

TWO: Oh right so you don't want me to be happy?

ONE: Please don't be like that.

TWO: Quick to judge though aren't you?!

ONE: Right, I'm done, just don't ask me my opinion in future.

TWO: So, at what point did I ask for your opinion?

ONE: Try to see the bigger picture.

TWO: Understandably, you're a bit jealous.

ONE: Very funny.

TWO: Why then are you being so negative?

ONE: (e)Xtra caution that is all, I'm worried about you.

TWO: You should just be happy that I've moved on and keep your opinion to yourself.

ONE: Zero opinion from now on!!!!

Physicality

Character two reacts to dialogue using only facial expressions and body language.

I have used these for TV acting classes and showreels for children. This dialogue could be recorded and played back for the students to react to; or played by another performer.

Try performing the following scenes in different ways, for the camera and for the stage. Discuss the main differences between the two performances.

Dialogue One

ONE: What did you say? Look at me child! What did you say? How dare you speak to me like that, who do you think you are? Look at you. Pathetic. Crying on the floor like a baby. You wouldn't have behaved like that if your mother had been around, would you? But she's not around, is she? And that's your fault. She left because of you. Are you listening to me, child? You are so pathetic. Look at me when I'm talking to you! How dare you turn away from your father! You're a disgrace.

Dialogue Two

(A person finds someone who looks lost and scared.)

PERSON: Are you ok?

STRANGER: *(Silent.)*

PERSON: Where do you live?

STRANGER: *(Silent.)*

PERSON: Would you like me to call someone?

STRANGER: *(Shakes head.)*

PERSON: What is your name?

STRANGER: (*Silent.*)

PERSON: Are you hurt?

STRANGER: (*Silent.*)

PERSON: I can't help you if you don't talk to me.

STRANGER: (*Mumbles name.*)

PERSON: Sorry?

STRANGER: (*Repeats name.*)

PERSON: What's your surname?

STRANGER: (*Shrugs.*)

PERSON: Is that your blood, (*name.*), are you hurt?

STRANGER: (*Shakes head.*)

PERSON: Can you stand?

STRANGER: (*Nods.*)

PERSON: Let me take you somewhere warm, it's cold out here and you're shivering.

STRANGER: (*Shakes head, panics.*)

PERSON: I'm not going to hurt you; I want to help. You can't stay out here all by yourself.

STRANGER: (*Reluctantly stands.*)

Chance Element

You will need a pack of playing cards.

Playing cards are given out to pairs or groups of students to decide on words that must be included in a scene. Have dictionaries available for students to look up the words.

They must include the words they've been given at random in their scene; it should seem natural, not forced.

Ace – Juxtaposition
Jack – Incredulous
Queen – Expedition
King – Gigantic
Joker – Composition
2 – Enlighten
3 – Ascertain
4 – Artificial
5 – Authoritative
6 – Exhilarating
7 – Admission
8 – Acrimonious
9 – Bourgeois
10 – Antidote

Playing cards to decide on location for a scene:

Ace – A luxury hotel
Jack – A tent
Queen – A lift
King – A car
Joker – A school
2 – A shop
3 – A changing room
4 – A fairy garden
5 – A castle
6 – An office
7 – A tropical island
8 – A train station
9 – A bus stop
10 – The beach

Playing cards are used for starting lines/ending lines/lines to be included in a scene:

Ace – It's the most amazing news.

Jack – If this is true, it's huge.

Queen – I don't believe you, he wouldn't…

King – But you said I was the winner.

Joker – If you take another step, you'll regret it.

2 – Stand still, really still.

3 – Snow White never had this problem.

4 – It's not exactly as it sounds.

5 – You can't tell her one thing and me another.

6 – What sort of question is that?

7 – Stop talking for a second.

8 – Are you seriously going to ask me to lie?

9 – I'm not going in first.

10 – I know you heard that too.

Playing cards used to set the rules for a scene (Four Players):

Ace – Can only say up to two words at a time.

Jack – The first thirty seconds must be mimed.

Queen – Player one must interrupt every line.

King – Player two must always be physically on a higher level.

Joker – The piece must have a comic element.

2 – Player four has a secret but it is never revealed.

3 –The scene takes place on a desert island.

4 – There is a disagreement, but it gets resolved.

5 – Player one agrees with everything that is said but can't use the word agree.

6 – Player two is a stranger to the other characters.

7 – Player three must have a translator.

8 – Four chairs must be used but never to sit on.

9 – Player four can only use one word at a time.

10 – The scene is set in a confined space.

You can reduce the options by using a dice instead of playing cards which might work better for younger students.

What's in the Box?

A scripted and spontaneous improvisation exercise.

Task One – Learn the dialogue below off by heart.

Task Two – The teacher will place a box in the centre of the performance space, when you get to the end of the dialogue the box is opened by character one. The rest of the scene is improvised, with reaction to the contents.

ONE: Where did you find it?

TWO: I can't tell you.

ONE: Why?

TWO: The less people know about it the better.

ONE: Are you telling me you just found it, or did you get it another way?

TWO: Are you suggesting I've done something wrong? Like illegal or something?

ONE: No, I just don't understand the big secret. Are you going to open it? Or do you already know the content?

TWO: Be patient.

ONE: Well if you're not going to open it then I will.

TWO: No don't...

(He/she opens the box, from here the scene is spontaneously improvised.)

Suggested Objects:

- Money
- Tool

- Flowers
- Item of clothing
- Blood-stained clothing or cloth
- Weapon
- Spectacles
- Book
- Blank DVD/CD
- Note saying 'I'm leaving'
- Mobile phone
- Magic wand
- Bible
- A pair of tights
- A present (There could be another prop planted inside this.)

Creating Your Own Dialogue for a Scene

Fill in the blanks then continue the scene.

A:

B: I found this.

A: Where?

B:

A: Really? Wow!

B: I know, I can't believe it.

A:

B:

A: I don't think you should keep it.

B:

A: Ouch

B:

A:

B: Are You kidding me?

A:

B: I thought you were my friend!

A: Did you?

B:

A:

B: See you.

A:

B:

A: I don't think that's right.

B: Did I ask for your opinion?

A:

B: Seriously stop interrupting.

A:

B:

A: I suppose you do have a point.

B:

A: Actually, I can't.

B: Why?

A:

B:

A: Okay.

B: It's not okay though, is it?

A: No, not really.

B:

A:

B: I was trying to help.

A:

B:

A:

B:

A: I'm going to stop you right there.

B: I was just telling you the truth.

A:

B:

A:

B: I can't help it, it's all true.

Alphabet Duologue

This can be used to work on different levels of exaggeration. Using a scale between one and ten, one being very understated, five being natural, and ten over exaggerated, ask performers to recite the alphabet below.

> **ONE:** A
>
> **TWO:** BC
>
> **ONE:** DEF
>
> **TWO:** G

ONE: HIJK

TWO: LM

ONE: NOPQ

TWO: RS

ONE: T

TWO: UVW

ONE: XY

TWO: Z

- Use levels of exaggeration to experiment.
- Add punctuation and create the conversation accordingly
- Decide what is happening between One and Two
- Prepare the scene but only using letters to communicate.
- Physicalise the scene. Can the class work out what is happening?
- Replace the letters with dialogue and perform the intended scene.

Improvisation Scenarios Based on a Given Theme

Choose a scenario as the starting point of a scene.

'Lost' Improv:

- Lost your mind
- Lost an important letter
- Lost a book
- Lost a diary
- Lost a pet
- Lost treasure
- Lost a friend

- Lost your way home
- Lost some money
- Lost a lottery ticket

'Stuck' Improv:

- Stuck on a rollercoaster
- Stuck in detention
- Stuck in a tree
- Stuck in an awkward situation
- Stuck in a lift
- Stuck on a desert island
- Stuck in a relationship
- Stuck in the mud
- Stuck in a hot air balloon
- Stuck in a time warp

Song Title

Using musical theatre song titles (or any genre of song) as a starting point for improvisation or devised works. The scene cannot have any reference to the musical it is from or use the same characters or storyline.

Some song title suggestions:

- Over the Rainbow
- Into the Woods
- Like No One I've Ever Seen
- Think of Me
- I Just Can't Wait to Be King
- Memory
- You Can't Stop the Beat

- Poor Unfortunate Souls
- One Day More
- Skid Row

Mimes

Solo mimes, performers can be asked at any moment to deliver a 'thought in the head' to ensure performers are in the mindset of the character.

All these scenarios can lead to duologue and group improvisations or be used as a starting point for monologue and script writing.

Waiting

1. You receive a present for your birthday which you absolutely hate; you pretend to love it.
2. You receive a nasty message on your phone from a bully.
3. You tell your mum a secret that has been on your mind.
4. You receive some bad news via a phone call.
5. You are in the dentist waiting room. You're due to have a tooth removed but you refuse to go in when your name is called.
6. You and your friend decide to explore the woods at night, you get lost and something spooks you.
7. You find yourself at Hogwarts, you have no idea how you got there.
8. You find an article about you in the newspaper.
9. Mime the event that led to the newspaper article.
10. You are at the centre of an incident at school.
11. You are in the wings waiting to go on stage, but you suddenly get a bad case of stage fright.

Mimes with a Chair

You are sat...

1. Waiting for a bus, you're going to be late.
2. Outside the teacher's office, you're in trouble.
3. In a very posh restaurant, you're not sure of the order you should use the cutlery.
4. Playing chess at the world championships.
5. Playing monopoly, you are cheating.
6. In an exam.
7. Presenting a children's TV show.
8. On the naughty step.
9. Feeling lonely in the playground watching other children play.
10. Waiting for your favourite pet to come out of the vets.
11. Waiting to find out if you have a new brother or sister.
12. Waiting for your date to turn up.

Cinema Reactions

The group sits in rows facing the front as if watching a cinema screen.

1. You are watching a happy film.
2. You are watching a scary film.
3. You are relieved when the superhero saves the day.
4. You don't understand what's happening.
5. You are enjoying the music in the film.
6. You are shocked by a sudden twist in the story.
7. You start to daydream about being in the film.
8. You are scared but trying not to show it.

9. You are trying to hold back tears and don't want anyone to know how the film has affected you.

10. It is the funniest film you've ever seen.

Christmas Themed Mimes

1. You get caught opening the presents under the tree before Christmas Day.

2. You pretend to be asleep on Christmas Eve and catch Santa coming down the chimney.

3. You are waiting in the wings to do your part in the nativity but you're so nervous.

4. You open a Christmas present from your auntie. It is an awful jumper, you try to fake excitement.

5. You wake up on Christmas morning at 3am and beg your parents to let you get up.

Improvisations Using Chairs

Use the scenarios below for spontaneous improvisation or prepared improvisation, along with one of the following rules:

1. You can only use questions in your dialogue.

2. You can only say a maximum of two words at a time.

3. Whatever happens B must always agree and go along with A.

4. The dialogue must follow the alphabet, each line starting with the next letter.

5. You must include a selected word. For this you can ask performers to write a word on a piece of paper and draw one out of a hat, use a random generator or my personal favourite a spinning wheel which you can get online and use whiteboard markers to write on it and then erase for multiple use.

Performer One – A

Performer Two – B

Scenario One

Starting position – A sat on a chair, B stood pointing at them.

Ending position – Both sat on chairs facing each other.

Scenario Two

Starting position – Both chairs laid on the floor, A and B enter stage left.

Ending position – A and B hold the chairs.

Scenario Three

Starting position – A is sat on a chair facing up stage, B enter stage right.

Ending position – A and B sat on the same chair.

Scenario Four

Starting position – A is asleep on a chair with feet outstretched on to another chair, B enters stage left.

Ending position – A and B sat astride the chair.

Scenario Five

Starting position – A is laid on the floor, B is sat on a chair looking down at B.

Ending position – A and B exit taking their chairs with them.

IMPROVISATION FOR LARGE GROUPS

Improvisation Game

The teacher gives a starting line. Students then step forward when they have a line to add. Their lines must begin with the first letter of their own name.

For Example:

JO: Just a minute, what do you think you're doing?

ANNIE: Actually, what I'm doing may well be of interest to you.

IAN: I doubt it.

WENDY: Well, I'm interested.

MIKE: Me too.

Styles

Take a starting line from *Short Scene Starters* on pages 34-36.

Teachers call out a style from the list below, or come up with their own, for performers to react to accordingly.

- Western
- Murder Mystery
- Musical
- Horror
- Pantomime
- Action Movie
- Rom Com
- Melodrama

The Party

A whole class improvisation. A host is chosen, and they begin the improv by setting up for a party. The teacher gives the rest of the class characters, traits and objectives.

Examples:

- You are a teenage girl, and your objective is to steal food without anyone noticing.
- You are a young celebrity, and your objective is to get some-one to say they love you.
- You are a nervous guest who speaks so softly it's inaudible.
- You are flirty, and fancy the host.

This could then be followed up with polished improvisations in small groups based on the characters from the party.

A variation of the above could have the teacher playing host and the students making up their own characters.

The Apocalypse

The classroom becomes a bunker, with the performers taking on the role of survivors. They are invited to enter the bunker when they feel ready and have established a suitable character in their minds.

Two confident performers are chosen to start the scene.

There should be a real emphasis on the idea that 'less is more.' It is not about stealing a scene or trying to add comedy. The scene should have a natural, realistic feel.

Over the years my students have loved taking part in this activity which, on occasion, has lasted a whole lesson. This very much depends on the performers' focus and ability to remain in role. Some of the strongest performances have come from performers who don't feel the need to speak, this includes a performer who remained in prayer the whole time and another who sobbed in a corner and panicked if anyone came close.

Added activities could include:

- A preparation lesson on developing the characters; including writing a monologue and a backstory. These could be shared, and the performers hot seated.

- During the improvisation the teacher can freeze the action and spotlight specific characters, bringing them to life whilst others mime around them.

- Thought tracking would be another useful tool here.

- Interior monologues are a useful tool to allow the performer to think more deeply about their role. During the improvisation, the teacher should ask students to stop the action and whisper the thoughts in their head. It doesn't need to be audible to others. After a minute or two the action resumes.

- Follow up lessons could include smaller group work; developing scenes from the characters' back stories pre-apocalypse or exploring what might happen if some of them leave the bunker.

- I have used this improvisation to create a series of episodes by using the last fifteen minutes of each session to improv the next part of the story, or a character's backstory.

- The exercise could lead to a scripted exercise. Below is an example of a script students could try as a follow up activity.

The Loft

Scene One

JEZ: I'm telling you I heard it on the news, the infection is heading this way. It started down south and is on its way to Yorkshire.

IAN: Are you kidding me?

JEZ: No I'm not, that's why we need to get the family together and make a space in the loft.

IAN: The loft?

JEZ: Yes, I figure we need to be high up. You know, in case of any manifestations.

IAN: Manifestations?

JEZ: Do I need to spell it out?

IAN: Erm, maybe.

JEZ: Zombie manifestations.

IAN: Zombie?

JEZ: This, Ian, is no normal infection! We are talking zombie apocalypse here.

IAN: Are you sure it was the news you were watching?

JEZ: Look, we are wasting time here. You gather as many bottles of water and tins of food as possible, don't forget the can opener. I'm on barricade duty, no sucker is getting anywhere near our loft. But look, you need to keep this quiet. The loft will only hold five people.

Scene Two

JEZ: And you chose to bring him because?

IAN: No one else would take me seriously.

JEZ: Jeez, Ian…how many people did you ask?

IAN: Terry was the fourth.

JEZ: Great, so when they all realise this is a real threat, they'll be fighting their way up here.

IAN: Sorry.

TERRY: I've always wanted a real-life adventure, Jez.

JEZ: Have you, Terry? Well isn't that great.

TERRY: Don't be like that, Jez, we're on the same side.

JEZ: You're a crazy loon, Terry.

IAN: Exactly, Jez; every zombie apocalypse has its batshit crazy character.

JEZ: This isn't a flaming comic book, Ian.

TERRY: I brought these (*He opens a case to reveal bows and arrows.*).

JEZ: A right modern-day Robin Hood you are (*Beat.*) Yeah, I guess you could be useful.

IAN: So what do we do now?

JEZ: Wait.

TERRY: Top Trumps, anyone?

IAN: Not now, Terry. I'm sure Jez has a plan he'd like to share with us.

Scene Three

(*They are playing Top Trumps.*)

IAN: So, mate, what did the news actually say? We've been up here four hours twenty minutes and thirty-five seconds and nothing seems to be happening.

JEZ: It started down south, Ian, the infections probably only just reached Birmingham. Zombies don't travel by car, Ian. Don't you watch The Walking Dead?

IAN: I'm still on season two.

TERRY: The Farm, that's the best one. I've watched them all and I don't actually remember at any point Rick saying, 'Come on, gang, let's hide in this loft!'

JEZ: Shut it, psycho.

IAN: Calm down.

JEZ: What did you bring him for?

IAN: I told you everyone else laughed.

TERRY: And I was just up for the laugh.

JEZ: You two morons will be laughing on the other side of your face when I kick your backsides down that hatch and into the clutches of some hungry Zombies.

IAN: Anyway, what happened to bringing your family?

JEZ: Changed my mind about asking them.

IAN: They laughed at you, didn't they?

JEZ: It's your turn (*Beat.*), it's your turn, Terry!

TERRY: Darth Maul power 270.

(*There's a sudden bang on the hatch. **TERRY** loads his bow with an arrow.*)

IAN: What the hell's that?

JEZ: They're here. This is it; they've got through the barricade.

HANNAH: Open the hatch, freaks.

JEZ: Hannah?

HANNAH: Jez, open the hatch.

(He lets her in, she looks around then bursts out laughing.)

HANNAH: Aww this is cute, Jeremy. Are you boys having a sleep over.

JEZ: Get lost.

TERRY: Hi, Hannah.

HANNAH: Get lost, Terry.

JEZ: What do you want?

HANNAH: I was bored, thought I'd come and see what my dozy brother and his dimwit mates were up to. Top Trumps, whoa party on, boys.

JEZ AND TERRY: Get lost, Hannah.

HANNAH: Oh, and Mum wants the can opener. So, these two numbskulls believed your story?

JEZ: You'll be sorry.

HANNAH: Sorry to be related to you.

JEZ: You can go now!

HANNAH: Hi, Ian.

IAN: Hey.

HANNAH: You want me to stay don't you, Ian.

IAN: Sure.

(Moaning can be heard.)

JEZ: Did you hear that?

TERRY: Yeah.

HANNAH: Was it you, Terry? Is that you belly rumbling?

JEZ: Shut up, Hannah. Ian, close the hatch, it's happening.

Task:

Devise a news bulletin based on the events Jez describes. This could include interviews with eyewitnesses, experts in virology, and survival tips.

Is what Jez is claiming true or an elaborate hoax? Devise the final scene.

Other stimuli for polished improvisation or devised performances:

- Ask performers to sketch a picture or write a sentence. Mix them up and give them to different groups as their starting point for a scene.
- Create a sculpture using random objects. Students to use the image as a starting point for discussion on what it means to them, then develop ideas into a scene.
- Existing artwork.
- Poetry (Performers could write their own.)
- Song lyrics.
- Historic events.
- Mythical stories.
- Photographs.
- Magazine articles.

Who Done It?

Scenario

A New Year's Eve party takes place. The teacher is the host. The teacher comes up with a character and tells everyone their profile.

E.g. My name is Annalise Monroe. I live in a mansion in a small quaint village called Beesford. I've never worked as my father gives me a substantial allowance, or he did until he passed away last year. He left me everything, the house, cars and millions of pounds. I'm 25 and I like to socialise, being popular is important to me so I'm going to host a big new years eve party and invite the whole village. (This character could potentially be given to one of the children to play.)

Plot

A party is held for all the villagers. On the stroke of midnight Annalise's body is found. For younger students perhaps it could be a thief they're looking for.

1. What sort of people might live in the village? Each person creates a character profile. This can be done in groups as they may decide that some are related etc. These are shared and the teacher makes notes on who is who etc.

2. Each group has a secret, decide what the secret is. Tell the teacher the secret but no other group can know.

3. Each person writes a short monologue set at home getting ready for the party, which gives the audience some insight as to who they are.

4. Teacher uses this information and the secrets to start generating a plot line.

5. Teacher decides who the murderer is, but doesn't reveal this.

6. In each session the teacher will group certain characters together and give them a scenario to create a scene, these will be performed at the end of each lesson. Gradually revealing clues.

7. At the end of each session the performers can hand in a piece of paper with who they suspect written on it. If they are correct you can either make a note but keep it secret until the big reveal and then tell them at the end who was first to get it right, or tell the performer they are correct and ask them to be in on the decisions for the plot. You could just say how many correctly guessed

at each stage.

8. You can conduct a hot seating of a character now and then to get more character info and plot ideas.

9. After some weeks of creating scenes you announce that in todays session the party and crime will take place. A whole class improvisation could be conducted. Everyone reacts to Annalise's death with a short monologue revealing who they suspect and why..

10. Teacher becomes the police detective and interrogates characters, everyone makes a final guess at who has done or before the detective reveals the murderer. It's a bit of planning for the teacher each week deciding on the plot line but they only need to be brief outlines. E.g. Suzy and Max have a disagreement with the local vicar who thinks they should be getting married in a church and not at Annalise's mansion.

Or

Terry who owns the shop takes Julie to one side and tells her he knows what she's up to. Julie then confronts Tom who she thinks has told Terry her secret.

Memories

Create areas in the space which are filled with stimuli from the past like a museum.

Area 1 – Old black and white photographs

Area 2 – Old postcards and letters

Area 3 – Old newspaper clippings

Area 4 – A time capsule or memory box containing interesting artefacts

Area 5 – A patchwork quilt, tell the students that each patch has a meaning/memory attached to it.

After spending some time exploring the areas, performers pick an item that interests them then tell the class why they chose it.

In groups choose an item as a starting point for a piece of drama. Performers are to create a freeze frame of a key moment, teachers are to thought-track the characters (This is where the teacher touches the shoulder of a performer who then speaks the line in their character's head). Performers then bring the scene to life. The thoughts in their head can be used as asides to the audience to create dramatic irony, allowing the audience to know something the other characters don't.

Stimuli for Devised Work

In groups, choose one of the three poems below and do the following:

- List words which are evoked from reading it.
- Devise a vocal performance of the chosen stimuli, the performance could include:
    1. A variety of dynamics
    2. Choral speaking
    3. Delivering words in canon
    4. Echoing of key words
    5. The most powerful line in the eyes of the performers could be repeated between other lines or verses.
    6. Consider sound effects
- Add choreographed movement to the vocal performance using unison and canon. Consider the use of background music.
- Spend some time discussing what the words mean and what

the writing is about, create a scene that best demonstrates
the key theme.

- Take moments from the scene and intersperse the vocal
performance with dialogue and action.

Poems

Using poetry as a stimulus for debate, devise scenes and monologues.

Capital Punishment

"The death sentence" the judge did say,
As the jury voted him dead,
And as they left the court in silence,
The criminal hung his head.

Led off to the chamber,
He pleaded "I'm insane",
But the executioner ignored him,
And he cried his last cry in vain.

He'd said his last prayer to God,
And forgiveness he had pleaded.
But was he really sorry for,
All the children he'd mistreated.

He had committed a serious sin,
But did he deserve to die?
Couldn't he just be jailed for life?
For this horrific and vulgar crime.

So, put this man to his death,
But surely that's a sin,
To have to lower yourself to this,
And commit the same crime as him.

Two wrongs don't make a right,
And if you murder this man,
Then do you deserve to die also?
Should this sentence be banned?

If you think the death penalty,
Will forever stop the crime,
Then you are sadly mistaken,
You should imprison for a lifetime.

No one has the right to take a life,
No matter what they've done,
There's more effective ways to solve,
The things we know are wrong.

Self-Destruction

There was a world that was created,
Many years ago,
That same world we destroyed,
As we watched the happiness erode.

And as we looked upon this slow death,
And watched the time tick by,
The world we took for granted,
Slowly withered and died.

No one really bothered to think,
Of the future it would hold,
And the children who would have to live,
In a world their parents sold.

The problems of the world,
We humans are aware,
But it's too late and all is lost,
Because no one really cares.

We had a selfish attitude,
Of wanting more and more,
Until we slowly did destroy,
The garden where we were born.

And because of greed and money,
With both we're always hooked,
We didn't stop to think,
One day we'd self-destruct.

And now that time has passed,
And the problems have arisen,
Our children have been born,
Into an environmental prison.

Where all they'll ever really know,
Of a world that was once great,
Is when their elders tell that ugliness,
Came when they tempted fate.

This is a story about the world,
And how you should think twice,
Before we all destroy the land,
With an evil man-made device.

And how a thought for the future,
Wouldn't be a thought to pass.
And a thought for our environment,
Would help to make it last.

Newspaper Headlines

For this activity the person or persons guessing could be students from the class, although I have done this using my class assistants instead of the students so they all get to act out the scenarios which have worked well.

Performers are told a newspaper headline that they must mime to the people who are guessing. The whole class perform at the same time until the headline is guessed correctly.

Here are some headlines to get you started.
"Technology banned in the UK"
"Tooth Fairy found to be real"
"Missing dog found on a boat"
"Devastating fire rips through Disneyland"
"Dragon ate my hat"

These headlines could then be a stimulus for the main lesson activity. E.g. creating a news report, creating a reconstruction of the event, chat show style interviews with those involved or eye witnesses, monologue writing.

Using Script Extracts as Stimuli for Devising Scenes

The Vermin Below

Scene One

IRIS: Mother, I can hear the mice again, I thought Dad put a trap out.

MOTHER: Just ignore them.

IRIS: They keep me awake.

MOTHER: You're always going to get mice in the country.

IRIS: Well I'm sure they'd rather be running free in the fields than running riot behind my skirting board.

MOTHER: I'll mention it to your father.

IRIS: Where is he?

MOTHER: He's working away for a few days.

IRIS: Nice of him to say bye.

MOTHER: He's a busy man.

IRIS: Why do you defend him? Can't you see how controlling he is?

MOTHER: He's just set in his ways.

IRIS: Well his ways dictate everything that happens in this house. What man doesn't allow his child to call their mother 'Mum'. Yet I can call him Dad.

MOTHER: You can call me Mum when he's away.

IRIS: You're missing the point. I'm going to meet Tom this afternoon.

MOTHER: I don't think it's a good idea. Your father will be upset.

IRIS: He's not here.

(*A scratching is heard.*)

IRIS: You see, did you hear that?

MOTHER: I don't think it's mice, probably just the house creaking.

IRIS: It's falling to bits this old place. Why can't we live in civilisation like the rest of the world. Oh wait, Dad doesn't like people.

MOTHER: Iris.

IRIS: I'll see you later.

Scene Two

*(**GIRL** is sat on a dirty old mattress holding a blood-stained blanket.)*

GIRL: Sometimes I think I hear your cry. I hold you in my arms and I believe I can see you, smell you. Then I look down and realise I am holding a blanket, I hold it tight and close to my heart because that is all that I have left of you. It is still bloodied from the day you were born, which reminds me you were real and that his accusations of my delusion are unfounded. My sanity is questionable, I know that to be true but who could forget giving birth, holding you, however short that moment may have been. He tells me I'm insane, that talking to you is unhealthy because he insists you don't exist. Did he take your life that day? Did you mean nothing to him? Tossed away like rubbish! It burns my head inside thinking such awful things. I need to believe you are alive, happy. I don't even know if you are a boy or a girl. It doesn't matter. Maybe you feel me in some way, a space in your heart you need filling but you don't know by who, or why. If I didn't talk to you there would be no point to my existence. I have lost track of time, I no longer scratch another day into the wall as night falls, in truth there is no space left on the wall. If I scratch it is to cause bleeding so that I feel pain, so that I feel something.

Scene Three

TOM: Did anyone see you?

IRIS: What do you take me for?

TOM: Are you sure about this?

Tasks:

- Read the duologue scene between Iris and her mother.

Create a role on the wall for each character.

- Draw or tape a line on the floor. Performers choose one of the two characters to play and stand on the line. The following questions are asked and performers decide if they are true or false statements. In role, the performers step in front of the line if it is true and behind if it is false. They can be asked 'Why?' at points during the exercise to encourage the performers to think more deeply about their character.

    1. I am sad more than I'm happy.
    2. I trust my family.
    3. I like living in the country.
    4. I feel listened to.
    5. No one understands me.
    6. I am scared of my father/husband.
    7. I have lived in this house my entire life.
    8. I have many friends.
    9. I have a secret no one knows.
    10. I think someone in my family has a secret.
    11. I'm anxious.
    12. I'm worried.

- The above task can be repeated for the characters of 'Girl' 'Tom' and 'Dad'.
- Use the task to further develop the role on the wall.
- Rehearse scene one. Freeze the scene at two different moments to get a 'thought in the head' of each character.
- Discuss the relationship between the characters of Iris and Mother. How does 'Dad' fit into the dynamic.
- Read the girl's monologue in scene two. Consider who she might be, how might she fit into the plot line?

- Practise and perform the monologue thinking about pace and vocal dynamics.

- Who might have been the last person to speak to the girl? Devise a duologue.

- Scene Three – Extend the scene where Iris meets Tom. Think about who he is and how he might fit into the plot line. What is his relationship to the other characters? What does the scene reveal?

- Hotseat Iris, Dad, Mother, Tom, Girl. Use this exercise to develop the characters and form devised scenes between;

  1. Iris and Dad

  2. Dad and Mother

  3. Iris, Dad and Mother

- There is also scope to do some monologue writing to further develop the characters and give the audience insight into their feelings. Read the monologue in scene two. Where is she? Is she isolated? Write a second monologue for the girl which develops the plot line. A possible plot line could be: A girl is being kept in the basement of their home by Iris's dad, who kidnapped her as teen. She is the birth mother of Iris. Her dad took the baby away at birth and she has been brought up unaware that the 'mother' upstairs is not her real mum. The girl (now a woman) scratches the wall in the basement which is what Iris hears believing it to be mice.

- Using the above plot line idea devise the following scenes:

  1. 'Girl's' parents the day she went missing.

  2. A news report and public plea from the parents of the missing teen.

  3. Girl and Dad the day the baby was taken upstairs.

  4. Mother and Dad the day the baby was taken upstairs.

(Does Mother know the truth about the girl in the basement?)

5. Iris and one of the other characters when she finds something that leads to suspicion that all is not what it seems in their family.

6. Iris finds the girl (now a woman).

7. Iris seeks help from her friend Tom. A subplot could be added here where it is revealed that Tom's aunt was the kidnapped girl.

8. The confrontation.

9. The girl/woman is finally freed. This might include an emotional reunion with the girl's parents, a news report and/or a police interview.

10. Iris and the girl/woman when it is revealed they are mother and daughter.

11. The aftermath. A split scene to show how the characters are coping.

• Performers can create a timeline of events and intersperse their devised scenes with monologues from the girl/woman in the basement to create a short play.

An alternative stimulus to the script extract could be the following short story extract:

"Mother, I can hear mice in the wall again. I thought Dad had put the traps out."

The constant scratching irritated her. It was worse at night-time. Her Dad would sort it and it would go quiet for a few days, then it would start up again. Those creatures are relentless.

Iris lives at Honey-Bee Farm, which sounds quaint and idyllic but in reality, it's a run-down building that's been in her family for years. She lived with her mother and Dad, they have lived there her whole life, except for the six months when her mother left, she disappeared one day, no note, nothing. Then re-emerged six months later with little explanation. Her dad wouldn't allow questions, just like he wouldn't allow her to call her mother 'Mum.' Iris just accepted the situation. The house is out in the sticks, no neighbours for two miles. Mother likes the peace, and Dad is a private person and doesn't have a need for social interaction. He doesn't like people much, not even Mother. Iris on the other hand feels total frustration with this isolated world they've created for her. She didn't mind when she was younger, playing in the fields was fun. Not so fun when you're fourteen.

Her closest friend lives in the village three miles from Honey-Bee Farm. His name is Tom and his dad used to work on the farm, until her dad decided he didn't need any help and fired him. The two families don't speak anymore but Iris's bond with Tom was too strong to break, so they meet in secret.

Themes that could be explored further during the devising process:

- Stockholm Syndrome
- Control
- Deceit
- Isolation
- Captivity

The Restaurant

*(We see **SIENNA** setting tables in the restaurant.)*

*(**JED** enters.)*

SIENNA: You're late.

JED: Who got out on the wrong side of the bed this morning?

SIENNA: At least I got out of bed this morning.

JED: Very funny.

SIENNA: How is the mystery woman?

JED: A mystery, so less of the questions.

SIENNA: What are you hiding?

JED: I just don't want to share my private stuff with everyone. Can you cover for me tonight?

SIENNA: No, Jed, we are both on the schedule tonight we are fully booked.

JED: Come on, Sienna, I've got a surprise date planned. Picture this, fairy lights, a secluded spot, champagne, moonlight...

SIENNA: Picture this, fifteen reservations, an angry manager, a stressed-out chef and one tired waitress. Now get your uniform on we open in ten minutes.

JED: Fine. I'll just have to let her down gently.

(*He begins to text.*)

SIENNA: What are you doing?

JED: Texting her.

SIENNA: Very gentle, Jed.

JED: She will be so upset.

SIENNA: I'm sure she will find something to do for one night without you.

JED: You've covered before.

SIENNA: And I can't keep covering, I'm not going to be here for ever, Jed. I've got plans you know, this is just temporary.

JED: You've been here three years!

SIENNA: Well, I'm just waiting for the right opportunity, aren't I? There's more to me than waiting on others and covering for you. And I'll have you know I got my first audition last week.

JED: For what? A speaking role?

SIENNA: Why does it matter it's still an audition.

JED: Yeah, but it could have been an audition for passer-by number two.

SIENNA: Actually, it was passer-by number one.

(*JED laughs.*)

SIENNA: Hey it's still a speaking role and all actors and actresses start at the bottom, it just makes eventually starring at the top that much sweeter.

JED: Okay, okay I'm proud of you. So how did it go?

SIENNA: Umm have you cleaned table nine.

JED: Seriously how did it go?

SIENNA: I don't think you've cleaned table nine.

JED: Did you get the part?

SIENNA: Oh look at that, it's time to open.

JED: Sienna.

SIENNA: Sorry, I can't hear you. Your first customers have come in. I better leave you to do your job.

(*She exits and returns with menus.* **WALTER** *enters with his imaginary wife.*)

JED: It's good to see you, Walter.

WALTER: I'm in every night, Jed, not seen you as often recently.

JED: Got myself a lady friend, Walt.

WALTER: You've got to keep them happy whilst you can, Jed.

JED: Good advice, how's Mavis this evening?

WALTER: Why don't you ask her yourself?

JED: Of course, how rude of me. How are you, Mavis? You look lovely tonight.

WALTER: She says thank you, Jed.

SIENNA: Hi, Walter, I've reserved your usual table for two. I've added a couple of extra flowers for you and Mavis. I heard on the grapevine it's a special occasion.

WALTER: Sixty years we've been married. You don't hear of that too often do you love.

SIENNA: You certainly don't. Let me show you and your lovely wife to the table.

(*SIENNA* guides *WALTER* to his usual table. The Robinson-Tate family enter.)

MR ROBINSON-TATE: We have a reservation for three, the Robinson-Tate family.

JED: Ah here you are, let me show you to your table.

(*They head to a table set for three.*)

MR ROBINSON-TATE: I specifically requested the window booth. We like our privacy.

JED: Oh I'm sorry the window seat has already been reserved and the gentleman is sat there about to order.

MR ROBINSON-TATE: He's sat alone taking up a larger table.

JED: He's a very special customer.

FELICITY: Daddy that old man is talking to himself.

MRS ROBINSON-TATE: Felicity don't be rude.

MR ROBINSON-TATE: Do you know who I am?

MRS ROBINSON-TATE: Stop making a fuss Ralph.

JED: Apologies, Mr Robinson-Tate but I can't ask Walter and his wife to move.

MR ROBINSON-TATE: His wife? Are you mocking me? That man is sat alone.

JED: That's a matter of opinion. I have another lovely table, very private.

MRS ROBINSON-TATE: Thank you that would be glorious.

MR ROBINSON-TATE: That is a matter of opinion.

Co-written by Abbi Mae Watkinson.

The tasks suggested for character development regarding *The Vermin Below* script would also work with this extract.

- Perform the extract adding regular asides from the characters, adding dramatic irony.

Suggestions for devised scenes:

- Sienna's audition.
- Jed on a date with his mystery woman.
- Flashback to three key moments in Walter and his wife's relationship before she passed away.
- Walter with his wife in her last moments.
- Walter alone after the passing of his wife. A day in the life of Walter.
- A day in the life of the Robinson-Tate family.
- A split scene demonstrating class divide between the characters.
- Create other customers to enter the restaurant, this could be done initially through spontaneous improvisation to generate ideas. Specific theme's, emotions or characteristics could be given out to inform the type of characters who enter the restaurant. Objectives could be decided on for

each character.

Theme's which could be explored further:

- Dreams and ambition
- Isolation and loneliness
- Love and relationships
- Class and status

Emotions could inform the scene as new characters enter, for example; frustration, dread, desire, anticipation, admiration, anger, anxiety, nervousness, satisfaction, uncertainty, confusion, paranoia, defensiveness.

The above emotions could be the atmosphere created during the scene or the feelings of an individual, they might also inform the characters objective.

Some examples:

- The character entering the scene might have an objective based on desire. Their objective being to gain the attention of another character romantically.
- Another might be 'anger' with the objective being the intention of getting a refund due to their dissatisfaction.
- Another might be 'dread' with the objective of meeting their partner in the restaurant to break up with them.

The following are suggestions for traits that could be given to the actors as they enter the scene as a new character:

- You are constantly on your phone
- You yawn every time someone speaks
- You only talk if it is to answer a question
- You are disinterested in what people are saying
- You tend to invade other people's space
- You are prone to exaggerating

- You only respond with one word at a time
- You are monotone
- You tend to respond emotionally to most situations
- You wear your heart on your sleeve
- You over gesticulate
- You have a short fuse
- You hesitate before replying to people when in conversation
- You are nosy and tend to be more interested in what is going on around you
- You are clumsy

Mud Sticks

*(The gender of **GARY** can be changed; the role of the solicitor is not gender specific.)*

*(**GARY** sits opposite a solicitor.)*

SOLICITOR: Did you intend to kill him?

*(**GARY** does not respond.)*

SOLICITOR: I can't help you if you don't talk to me.

*(**GARY** remains silent.)*

SOLICITOR: Gary, I need to build a case for you, and I can only do that with your cooperation.

*(**GARY** stares at his solicitor.)*

SOLICITOR: You confessed to the detective. Did you intend to kill him?

GARY: No!

SOLICITOR: But you did intend to hurt him.

GARY: No, I don't know, not really.

SOLICITOR: Not really?

GARY: I didn't even really know him, it was just a laugh, a stupid joke.

SOLICITOR: A joke? Gary a man is lying dead in the morgue.

GARY: I know.

SOLICITOR: You have to be totally up front with me if I am to represent you. I need to know as much about you as possible.

GARY: There's not a lot to know.

SOLICITOR: What about your family?

GARY: Keep them out of it!

SOLICITOR: I need to know what your upbringing was like.

GARY: What the hell has that got to do with this?

SOLICITOR: I need to paint a picture of you in court, of your life. It could help your case.

GARY: My case? Or my sentence?

SOLICITOR: Tell me about your Dad.

GARY: He wasn't my Dad.

SOLICITOR: Oh, I thought...

GARY: He was my father, not my Dad.

SOLICITOR: There's a difference?

GARY: This conversation's over, I want to go back to my cell.

This script can be used as a starting point for a devised piece of drama. A useful technique would be flash forwards and flash backs to explore Gary's back story whilst exploring what the future may hold for this character.

Questions to consider:

- How old is Gary?
- Who is the victim?
- Is Gary guilty?
- What was his home life like?

Suggested scenes to devise:

- A family scene when Gary was a child
- The day before the crime
- The crime
- The day after the crime
- Police interrogation
- The court case
- The first night in prison

Themes to explore:

- Crime
- Nature versus nurture
- Isolation
- Revenge
- Justice

WORKING WITH SCRIPT

Attention to Detail

I use this exercise to demonstrate the importance of focus and attention to detail when putting on a play or working with script. However, I only tell them the purpose of the exercise at the end of the task, and only after asking them what they think it was about.

Performers are asked to take a walk around the room, touching each of the four walls. They are asked to think about:

a. How they walk, the style and speed.

b. How they touch the wall, softly, aggressively etc.

c. Which part of the wall they touch.

d. Who they walk past.

e. Whether they have any eye contact with anyone on their short journey, and if so, how do they react.

f. What order they arrive back at their starting point.

After the performers complete their journey, they are asked to describe it. Then they are asked to repeat the journey exactly as they had done before with attention to detail. On their return, the differences are discussed.

They are asked to repeat the journey one more time giving greater attention to the subtleties of their journey. This is then discussed in relation to the importance of focus and detail when portraying a character in a play; be it in relation to characterisation or following stage direction.

I would use this exercise before blocking a scene for the first time.

Animating Characters

The following extracts are taken from the play *Little Bo Peep and the Report of the Missing Sheep.*

These extracts can be used for character work in class, including work on caricatures, stereotypes and exaggeration. They also make useful audition pieces for the play.

Task:

Choose from an extract below and decide which character to play. Walk around the room in role. Teacher can use a scale from one to ten (five being natural) to allow performers to feel the change in their physicality during this exercise.

Performers greet each other in character. At first with just one word, then two, three, and so on - including larger than life gestures.

Explore status. Performers introduce themselves in character, then stand in a line in order of status, from lowest to highest. Discuss why they have chosen that position in the line and how they can show their status on stage. Does their stage status ever change?

Run scenes using physicality only. Can we understand the characters feelings through movement, gesture and facial expressions alone?

Performers rehearse and perform the scene; considering physicality, vocal qualities, levels of exaggeration and status.

The following short extracts have been selected with pre-teens in mind. However, the play is suitable for early teens as well. They are not the full scenes and are not necessarily in the order of the play.

Extract One

QUEEN OF HEARTS: Do not touch my tarts!!

(*To audience.*) Do you hear me?! They are for someone very special...

KNAVE OF HEARTS: Who, Your Majesty?

QUEEN OF HEARTS: Me!

KNAVE OF HEARTS: Would you mind if I tasted one? I've heard great things about your jam tart recipe.

QUEEN OF HEARTS: From whom? I have never shared my recipe with anyone!!

KNAVE OF HEARTS: From you.

QUEEN OF HEARTS: Ah yes, it's true my recipe is the best in the land.

Extract Two

BO: Hello, Humpty.

HUMPTY: Oh hi, Bo, how are you this fine day?

BO: I'm ever so worried Humpty, it's not like my Baabra and Baartie to wander off like that. Baabra doesn't like the cold and she will be so frightened, and Bartholomew is afraid of the dark. They must be found before the sun goes down. I thought you might be able to see them from your wall.

HUMPTY: Sorry, Bo. I haven't seen them I'm afraid.

BO: Please will you keep a look out for them and let me know egg-sactly where I can find them?

HUMPTY: Was that an egg joke?

BO: Oh no, Humpty, it wasn't an egg joke. I wouldn't be yolking at a time like this.

(BO giggles.)

MISS MUFFET: Oh hi, Bo, you're up early.

WILLIE: Why are you so sad?

BO: I've lost my sheep, Willie.

WILLIE: You've got a sheep called Willie?

BO: No, Willie, that's your name. I was addressing you.

WILLIE: Oh, I see. Sorry, Bo it's been a long night.

BO: It's Baabra and Baartie, they've disappeared and they're not the type to wander from the field.

MISS MUFFET: That's terrible, Bo. Move up, Willie let Bo sit down. Would you like to share my curds and whey?

BO: That's very kind of you, Miss Muffet, but I need to continue with my search. I must find them by nightfall; Baartie is scared of the dark.

Extract Three

QUEEN OF HEARTS: Where have you been, brother dearest?

KING COLE: I had an appointment.

QUEEN OF HEARTS: All appointments go through me.

KING COLE: I'm still the king…unfortunately. I'm just on a break.

QUEEN OF HEARTS: Then take a break and stop getting under my feet. No one needs to see that miserable face. I've got a bake off to win. Pass me the flour.

KING COLE: Maybe you should be thinking less about your tarts and more about running the land fairly and with compassion. Bo's sheep are still missing; maybe you can assist Duke with the investigation.

QUEEN OF HEARTS: That's where you went wrong, dear brother. Where did compassion get you? I don't assist anyone. I only have assistants.

KING COLE: Fine, have it your way, I haven't got the energy. I've got the season finale of *Stranger Things* to catch up on.

QUEEN OF HEARTS: Do not touch my tarts!

Extract Four

BO: Good morning, Mary.

MARY: Is it?

BO: Well now you mention it, no, not really. Are you ok? How does your garden grow?

MARY: Are you joking, Bo? No, I am not okay Bo. Look at my garden. Vandals, I tell you. Vandals!

BO: Oh my, it is a bit of a mess.

MARY: This is the work of stray sheep, Bo, hungry sheep.

BO: You said vandals.

MARY: Hungry vandals of the four-legged kind.

BO: I really don't think sheep would or could make this kind of mess.

MARY: What do you know? Word is that you've neglected your sheep and they've run away. They're probably famished, wouldn't you say, Bo?

BO: No, I wouldn't say, Mary, and I think you're very rude and somewhat lacking in sensitivity.

MARY: And I think you know exactly where Baabra and Baartie are. I wouldn't put it past you to be harbouring criminals.

BO: That's it, I've had enough of this.

Extract Five

DUKE: Maggie, can you explain why your children's clothes are all made of wool?

MAGGIE: I didn't realise it was a crime to wear woollen garments. Johnny, get off of Liza!

JOHNNY: She hit me first.

MAGGIE: I don't care, get off of your sister.

LIZA: Mum, he hit me.

DUKE: Control your children, Miss, please.

MAGGIE: Kids, sit down and let this fine gentleman speak.

DUKE: Gentleman, eh?

MAGGIE: May I just say, Duke, you're looking more handsome with age.

(He is flattered and takes out his mirror to admire himself.)

DUKE: Handsome?

MAGGIE: Oh yes, very.

DUKE: Well, I guess there is something about…wait you're side-tracking me. That's very devious.

*(**MAGGIE's** mischievous children are running riot in the station.)*

MAGGIE: Kids, leave that Kingsman alone. (**MAGGIE** flirts with **DUKE**.). It's only devious if it's untrue, Dukey.

Extract Six

BO: Wow, Mr Cow, you're in good shape.

MR COW: Thanks, Bo, I've been training hard. I've got the Animalympics coming up and I've been picked for the Nursery Rhyme team.

BO: I heard, it's fantastic news. It's a shame Baartie might miss it, he was selected too. Poor Baartie, he must be so scared.

MR COW: I know Bo; I hope he's found soon.

BO: Anyway, congratulations on your recent record for jumping over the moon, that's very impressive.

MR COW: Oh thanks, Bo.

BO: Aren't you happy?

MR COW: Yes of course, I am proud of myself but Baartie was meant to be attempting the record too. It felt wrong to take part without him.

Extract Seven

QUEEN OF HEARTS: I said don't touch my tarts! Where's the knave? He's supposed to be watching them.

WILLIE: I'm sorry I only had a nibble.

(He begins to dramatically choke. Everyone stops what they are doing and gathers round.)

MISS MUFFET: We need medical attention. Is there a doctor in the house?

DOCTOR FOSTER: Coming through.

MISS MUFFET: With all due respect Doctor Foster, you're a therapist.

DOCTOR FOSTER: I think he's…

MARY: You can't talk him back to life, or maybe you can. No, you definitely cannot.

MISS MUFFET: He's not dead, he's…

WILLIE: Winding you up.

QUEEN OF HEARTS: That is a cruel trick, Willie Winkie.

WILLIE: They're actually very tasty. Maybe now you can be less possessive and learn to share.

Ghosts

*(**MICHAEL** and **JESS** are exploring the woods and find a spooky looking house.)*

MICHAEL: Let's go!

JESS: Where are we going, Mike?

MICHAEL: I've told you we're going to the woods.

JESS: Can't we go somewhere else?

MICHAEL: Are you scared?

JESS: No... I just get bored listening to your stupid ghost stories.

MICHAEL: Do you want to hear one now...

JESS: No!

MICHAEL: They're true you know; Dad says.

JESS: I don't want to go, Michael. Mum said we had to be home by six.

MICHAEL: You're such a scaredy-cat! Look, I brought Dad's camera, if we can get a picture of the ghost we'll be famous!

JESS: I don't want to be famous; I just want my tea.

MICHAEL: What's that?

JESS: What?

MICHAEL: The smoke coming from that house? It's meant to be empty!

JESS: Mikey, we have to go home.

*(**MICHAEL** has already walked towards the house.)*

JESS: Mikey, stop. Where are you going?

MICHAEL: Come on, Jess, keep up. We haven't got all day!

JESS: Michael!

MICHAEL: Jess!

JESS: Argh! You are going to get us in so much trouble.

*(**JESS** reluctantly follows. They approach the big wooden door of the abandoned house.)*

JESS: Come on, let's go back home!

*(**MICHAEL** knocks on the door. The door opens but there is no one there.)*

MICHAEL: Well, that was creepy.

JESS: That's why I think we should leave.

*(**MICHAEL** enters.)*

MICHAEL: Hello! Anyone here? Hello.

(A swoop of wind slams the door behind them. Lights come up on a couple by a log fire.)

HENRY: Did you hear that, love?

LIZA: It's just the wind, Henry.

HENRY: No, I think it was the door.

LIZA: You've got a vivid imagination, Henry. It's windy out there tonight.

JESS: Ssh! Mikey, there's someone in here.

MICHAEL: I know, I told you...ghosts!

JESS: Pack it in, you're scaring me now.

HENRY: I'll check it out.

MICHAEL: I'll check it out.

JESS: Don't leave me here.

LIZA: Henry, it's nothing relax.

Task:

After reading the script, create a role on the wall for each character. The teacher should lead a hot seating activity, to give insight into each character's thoughts and fears.

The teacher should give performers some special effects to add to the scene to create atmosphere. Alternatively, a soundscape could be created by the performers themselves.

The performers could use physical theatre to create objects in the scene, e.g. becoming the door, or trees in the woods.

Who are Henry and Liza? Could there be a twist to the story? Performers can create their own concluding scene.

Up High

(Two friends are stuck at the top of a rollercoaster. These could be any combination of gender and the names changed accordingly.)

AMY/ANDY: I knew it, I just knew it.

LISA/LEE: Give it a rest.

AMY/ANDY: It's okay for you to say, you're not the one with a fear of heights. This is all your fault. You made me get on.

LISA/LEE: I can't physically make you get on anything.

AMY/ANDY: You bribed me.

LISA/LEE: I offered to buy you lunch, that's not a bribe! It is merely a kind gesture from one friend to another. Now calm down.

AMY/ANDY: I am calm...oh my days, oh my days. There's a wasp.

LISA/LEE: Where?

AMY/ANDY: It's buzzing in my ear. Waft it, don't hit it. You'll make him angry. Just waft it away. It's on me, it's on me! Help! Help me!

LISA/LEE: You need to chill.

AMY/ANDY: It's on me, get it off! Get it off!

LISA/LEE: Just sit back and enjoy the view.

*(**LISA/LEE** slaps **AMY/ANDY's** leg.)*

LISA/LEE: There got it.

AMY/ANDY: Ow! It stung me. What if I'm allergic and blow up like a balloon?

LISA/LEE: Then you can float down.

AMY/ANDY: That's not funny.

LISA/LEE: Will you just stop being so dramatic, sit back enjoy the beautiful view and wait for assistance.

AMY/ANDY: View of what? The clouds, the treetops? It's not a view I want to experience. Oh jeez, is that a man climbing up the track?

LISA/LEE: You see, a rescue party.

AMY/ANDY: Hardly. Who does he think he is Spiderman? How is one man going to get this great big carriage down? He's more likely to fall to his doom. Oh my goodness we all are. We are facing imminent death! Help us!

LISA/LEE: You need to breathe!

AMY/ANDY: I am! I think, maybe I'm not. Lisa, I can't breathe, I can't breathe! There's no air, I'm choking.

LISA/LEE: No you're not. Look here's a fire engine.

AMY/ANDY: Oh no, we're on fire too?

LISA/LEE: Of course not, they've come to get us down.

AMY/ANDY: How is that ladder going to reach up here?

LISA/LEE: Look there's a team of people down there trying to get it started.

(The girls jolt forward.)

AMY/ANDY: We moved. I don't want to move.

LISA/LEE: I thought you wanted to get down.

AMY/ANDY: That was before I remembered we haven't done the loop the loop yet.

LISA/LEE: Hold on tight!

*(**LISA/LEE** throws her hands in the air and cheers with delight, **AMY/ANDY** holds on to the carriage and screams.)*

Task:

Play a game of Pass the Movement. A movement is passed around the circle in canon. Each performer gets a turn to change it.

1. Play a clip of a rollercoaster in action (there are plenty to choose from on YouTube). Performers sit on chairs facing the screen and move in unison to the movements of the ride, as a physical theatre introduction to their scene. If a screen is not possible then performers can choreograph the movement. This can often work better in pairs, with each pair teaching the class their short phrase to create one long physical sequence for the whole group to perform in unison.

2. Create a whole group role play by following this process.

3. The class mimes getting into the carriage and adds sound effects using voice to represent the safety bar coming down. They enact their roller coaster movement sequence.

4. One performer is chosen to be the reluctant rider (R.R) and the following dialogue takes place:

> **R.R:** I don't like this.
>
> **All:** You'll be fine.
>
> **R.R:** My safety bar is loose.
>
> **All:** You'll be fine.
>
> **R.R:** I want to get off!
>
> **All:** Too late. Here we go!
>
> **R.R:** Oh no!!

5. Then the performers follow the rollercoaster's directions on the film through mime and add vocal sound effects, e.g. Ah, Ooh etc.

6. Each performer decides on a line to shout out as the ride is moving, these are added to the movement sequence.

7. Performers break off into pairs to write four to eight lines of dialogue which will be added into the performance.

8. Performers read the script and discuss how it would feel to be stuck on a ride. This scenario can then be added to the class performance using the script extract or their own version.

9. Finally, the ride moves again and draws to an end. Performers mime getting out of the carriage and they each get a final line as they exit the stage.

Fairy Tale Land News Bulletin

NEWSREADER: Good evening from FTL news at ten. We start our bulletin tonight with the trial of the big bad wolf. There's been a huge twist in this already dramatic story. We go over to our Fairy

Tale Land correspondent who is outside the court house. Good evening Giles/Gillian can you fill us in on this afternoon's events?

GILES/GILLIAN: Good evening, yes well as we all know the big bad wolf has been on trial for criminal damage and arson after destroying three homes all belonging to the three little pigs. I have Mr Wolf's lawyer with me today. Welcome Mr/s Vine, what was the atmosphere in court today?

MR/S VINE: It was electric, finally the truth is being revealed.

GILES/GILLIAN: And what is that truth?

MR/S VINE: My client has endured years of persistent bullying from those pigs.

GILES/GILLIAN: So he destroyed their houses in revenge?

MR/S VINE: No, he was set up. The pigs wanted him sent to jail, they set the whole crime up. Mr Wolf is the victim here. That's all I have to say on the case.

(***PIG ONE*** *walks past.*)

GILES/GILLIAN: Thank you for your time Mr/s Vine.

(*MR/S VINE exits.*)

GILES/GILLIAN: Hey Mr Pig, one minute... Mr Pig... FTL News... do you have any comments?

PIG ONE: That wolf did not get the title 'Big Bad' for no reason. It's lies all lies! He needs to be locked away.

GILES/GILLIAN: I believe a witness has come forward to say they saw you and your gang at the scene of the crime looking suspicious.

PIG ONE: Of course we were there, we live, or should I say lived there.

GILES/GILLIAN: What is your opinion on the accusation of persistent bullying?

PIG ONE: No comment.

GILES/GILLIAN: Back to the studio.

NEWSREADER: Thank you Giles/Gillian. We will update you after tomorrow's day in court. It's like a TV drama, so many twists and turns. In other news Goldilocks is charged with breaking and entering and a serious abuse charge has been brought against Cinderella's step mother. More on that after the commercial break when we have an exclusive from Cinderella herself.

Task:

There is an opportunity to devise fairy tale themed commercials. For example: gingerbread houses, the latest fashion... glass slippers, stranger danger warning from Red Riding Hood, porridge, magic beans.

NEWSREADER: Welcome back. Earlier this morning we managed to get an exclusive interview from Cinderella after her horrific ordeal.

INTERVIEWER: Thank you for talking to us today Cinderella.

CINDY: You can call me Cindy, my stepmother would yell 'Cinderella do this, Cinderella do that' I'd rather be known as Cindy from now on. You know, like a fresh start.

INTERVIEWER: Okay, Cindy. Can you tell us about your ordeal?

CINDY: My stepmother hated me. She would treat me as a slave, I had to do chores day and night and play servant to my stepsisters.

INTERVIEWER: That sounds awful. Were you scared of her?

CINDY: Yes. If I didn't do the chores correctly she would lock me in the cellar for days. I had mice to keep me company.

INTERVIEWER: That can't have been nice having mice crawling around.

CINDY: Oh no that was the thing that kept me going, the mice were my friends.

INTERVIEWER: Do you hope for a prison sentence?

CINDY: I don't wish her to be sent to prison but I would like her to get community service, doing chores herself!

INTERVIEWER: On a positive note, we hear that you've had contact from the palace and that the prince would like to meet you.

CINDY: We have already met on the one occasion when I escaped from my stepmother with the help of my fairy godmother. So, I guess you could call this a second date.

INTERVIEWER: Wait...fairy godmothers exist?

CINDY: Oh yes, but they like to keep a low profile.

INTERVIEWER: We wish you well Cindy, thank you for talking to us today. Back to the studio.

NEWSREADER: You heard it here first. Fairies do exist! More on this on tomorrow's news bulletin. Good night.

Task:

Devise tomorrow's bulletin with the exclusive "Fairies do exist."

Other activities could include:

- List all the incidents in well-known fairy tales that are crimes. For example, witch attempting to murder and eat Hansel and Gretel.

- Write a script like the example here reporting on other fairy tale crimes.

- Court room dramas.

- Chat show style scenarios to discuss issues raised e.g. do fairies exist?

The Magic Bookcase

(Four children are visiting their grandma, she lives in a big old house. During a game of hide-and-seek, they discover a magic bookcase which introduces them to new adventures.)

(This could be used as it stands, or as a classroom activity where the children can add scenes which are linked to their favourite books.)

Scene One

JUDY: This house kind of spooks me.

JO: It's just old, like Grandma.

ELSIE: We should explore.

JUDY: But Grandma said we shouldn't run around in case we break something.

TOM: Or in case we find something more like.

JO: I can't see what we would find that would be of interest.

ELSIE: Treasure!

JUDY: You're not going to find any treasure in here, just a load of spiders.

TOM: I love spiders.

JUDY: Well I don't!

JO: How about hide-and-seek?

TOM: Good idea, I'll count.

JUDY: I'm not hiding anywhere in this place.

ELSIE: Don't worry, Judy, you can come with me.

TOM: One, two, three, four…

(Blackout.)

TOM: Coming, ready or not.

JUDY: Well that's me caught.

TOM: I thought you were hiding with Elsie.

JUDY: So did I, but she ran off and hid in that big old chest, I bet it's full of spiders.

ELSIE: Hey! You're not supposed to tell.

JUDY: Sorry.

TOM: Come on, let's find Jo.

JUDY: I know where she is too.

TOM/ELSIE: JUDY!

JUDY: Ok, I won't tell. But you're very cold.

TOM: We're coming to find you, Jo.

(Blackout.)

TOM: Ok, Judy, you can tell us now. It's been half an hour and I've been in every room.

JUDY: No you haven't.

ELSIE: What do you mean?

JUDY: Didn't you see that bookcase in the library?

TOM: Yes, but we've been there.

JUDY: But you haven't been *in* there.

ELSIE: In the bookcase?

JUDY: Yes, I've seen it in films. You pull back a book and hey presto.

ELSIE: That's in the films, Judy, not real life.

JUDY: I saw her. Jo pulled back a copy of *Mother Goose* and in she went.

TOM: Fine, if you're so sure lead the way.

(Blackout.)

JUDY: Here we are. Look, here it is. Pull it, Elsie.

ELSIE: Ok, but I think this is your vivid imagination talking.

(The bookcase opens and a goose flaps past startling them.)

TOM: What on earth is this place? And what was that?

ELSIE: Not sure it is on Earth, Tom.

JUDY: It was a goose, like in the story.

TOM: What story?

JUDY: Mother Goose, the book that opened the entrance to this place.

TOM: What? So, you think we have stepped into the story?

JUDY: Maybe.

ELSIE: Look there's Jo.

JUDY: And she's carrying a…

JUDY/ELSIE/TOM: Golden egg!

JO: Thought you guys would never find me. Look at this.

ELSIE: Told you we'd find treasure.

JO: We found a bit more than that.

TOM: Let's go back through the bookcase and pull a different book, maybe it affects this place.

JUDY: As long as we stay away from those Greek myth books.

TOM: Why?

JUDY: I don't fancy meeting the Hydra.

(Blackout.)

Scene Two

(They are back in front of the bookcase.)

ELSIE: Let me choose, I think I'll have this one…

Task:

In groups, performers discuss their favourite books, stories, rhymes and myths. Then choose one to explore further. Create a series of freeze frames (tableaux) that tell the story frame by frame. Use this sequence of events to continue from Elsie's final line. As the characters re-enter the bookcase, devise scene two which integrates the characters in this extract with the characters from your chosen story.

Comparing Scene Extracts

Read the following two scenes, what do they have in common?

The Piano Exam

(Two children are sat in a room waiting to take their piano exam.)

WILLIAM: Hi, my name's William.

JOE: Hi, Will.

WILLIAM: No, it's William. My mum thinks shortening names is common.

JOE: Oh, right. My name's Joe, short for Joseph.

WILLIAM: Oh, right.

(Awkward silence.)

WILLIAM: Have you been playing the piano long?

JOE: Started this year.

WILLIAM: Oh, you must be fairly good to take an exam so soon.

JOE: It's just Grade 1.

WILLIAM: Ah yes, that was a pretty easy grade. I took that when I was only six; they call me a prodigy. I'm doing Grade 7.

JOE: Wow that's good!

WILLIAM: You seem nervous.

JOE: I'm terrified.

WILLIAM: You'll be fine, just warm up your fingers like this. (*He wiggles his fingers in a bizarre exercise routine.*)

WILLIAM: Go on, you try.

JOE: The receptionist is giving you a funny look.

WILLIAM: Just try it, my private tutor insists on it and it works for me; six distinctions so far. Go on, like this.

(*JOE reluctantly joins in.*)

JOE: To be honest it's just making my hands ache.

WILLIAM: Where do you take lessons?

JOE: My grandpa teaches me. He has this great big old keyboard at his house.

WILLIAM: Keyboard? Oh that's interesting. My parents just bought me a grand piano which we have pride of place in our music room.

JOE: You have a music room?

WILLIAM: Yes, it's important to have a place to express yourself.

JOE: My grandpa's keyboard is in his living room. He likes to watch the news at the same time. He says it's important to keep up with what's going wrong in the world.

WILLIAM: That would hinder my concentration.

JOE: Well I'm just a beginner so I don't mind.

(Silence, JOE looks nervous.)

WILLIAM: Are you ok? You look a little pale.

JOE: I'm just a bit worried I will hit a bum note.

WILLIAM: It's a learning curve.

JOE: Yeah sure, a learning curve.

WILLIAM: I think they called your name.

JOE: Really?

WILLIAM: No, I'm just jesting, lightening the mood a little.

JOE: That's not very funny.

WILLIAM: Sorry.

JOE: I'm just going to look at my sheet music, get it firmly in my head.

WILLIAM: Oh I don't need to do that, when I start playing it just happens. Electricity just flows from my brain to my fingertips. It's like magic.

JOE: Sounds it. Do they call you Harry?

WILLIAM: No, I told you my name's William.

JOE: It was a joke.

(WILLIAM looks confused.)

JOE: Harry Potter.

WILLIAM: Oh, I don't have time for films or jokes for that matter.

*(**JOE** goes back to reading his sheet music.)*

WILLIAM: What pieces are you playing?

JOE: Minuet in C and The Lonely Road.

WILLIAM: Well, they're nice and simple for someone inexperienced like you, you'll be fine. I'm playing Andante second movement from Sonata in G, and Cancion de Cuna from Suite de Pequeñas Piezas.

JOE: Sounds difficult to say, let alone play.

WILLIAM: Not for someone like me.

JOE: Of course not.

WILLIAM: I'm rather looking forward to showing off my skills to the examiner. You'll probably go in before me, being that you're on a lower grade.

JOE: Good, I want to get it over with.

WILLIAM: You should enjoy the moment; musicianship is a gift from God.

JOE: I think my gift came from my grandpa.

(Silence.)

JOE: Wait did that lady just call your name?

*(**WILLIAM** looks sheepish.)*

WILLIAM: I don't think so.

JOE: Is your last name Anderson-Smith?

WILLIAM: Might be.

JOE: Well she just said William Anderson-Smith grade *one* piano.

WILLIAM: I think you misheard I'm on grade seven, *se-ven!* Not one.

JOE: Sure you are.

WILLIAM: I am, I'll just correct her when I get inside.

JOE: Yes, you do that. Suddenly I don't feel quite so nervous. Good luck, Harry. You might want to take your wand; something tells me you might just need it.

*(**WILLIAM** leaves and **JOE** shakes his head and laughs.)*

More Dragons

*(**ROB** has moved schools and **TOM** has been designated to look after the new boy and give him a tour of the school.)*

TOM: Hey, I hear you've moved down here from London. My name is Tom. Mr Woods asked me to show you around today and make you feel welcome.

ROB: That's great, just great. I'm really glad to be here.

TOM: Really?

ROB: No not really. I went to the best school London has to offer. My chance of a promising high-flying career was, well quite frankly, off the scale. It was inevitable that one day I would follow in my father's footsteps.

TOM: Ah well I'm sure your brain hasn't shrunk, and you've probably got the same chance of getting top grades here.

ROB: I doubt that.

TOM: Alrighty then. Shall we start at the English block?

ROB: If you like.

TOM: So this is our library, it's got most of the best-selling books in here so there's always something good to read.

ROB: My dad's an author; he's won awards and everything. That's how he made his millions.

TOM: Wow, what books did he write?

ROB: Nothing you'd have heard of, they're to do with neuroscience and astrophysiology. You know, clever stuff.

TOM: Have you read them?

ROB: Of course. I contributed to the research.

TOM: Really?

ROB: Yes. I'm a member of Mensa.

TOM: Of what?

ROB: A society for geniuses.

TOM: Ah okay. I guess you'll be in set one then.

ROB: I would certainly hope so.

TOM: Isn't astrophysiology basically to do with star signs?

ROB: Sorry?

TOM: Star signs you know, Scorpio, Aquarius, Gemini…

ROB: There's much more to it than that!

TOM: Anyway, moving on. To your right is the gymnasium where we have P.E.

ROB: I was in my school's football team. Top scorer in every match. My dad knows David Beckham.

TOM: Of course he does.

ROB: He does. I went to school with his son.

TOM: And I bet he was your best friend.

ROB: One of them, I had loads of friends. They're all really missing me.

TOM: I bet they are. Anyway, if we just turn this corner we find the languages block.

ROB: I'm multilingual. I can speak five languages fluently. Probably because I've travelled the world.

TOM: With your dad?

ROB: Yeah, he's like a travel correspondent for the BBC.

TOM: Is that between writing top books on super intelligent stuff?

ROB: He writes as we travel from country to country.

TOM: He's a busy man.

ROB: Very. He's working in London though at the moment giving the Prime Minister advice.

TOM: Advice on what?

ROB: Oh, everything he needs advice on, which is quite a lot. He knows everything about everything my dad. You know all the super clever important stuff anyway.

TOM: Right. Well let's have a quick look at the music room. Do you play an instrument? I play drums.

ROB: I've been learning piano since I was two, guitar since I was 3 and drums since I was 4. I'm basically a one-man band.

TOM: Think it might be more fun to be in a band with other people.

ROB: My dad says, 'Why would you want to work with others when your talent will only make them feel inadequate?'

TOM: That's very thoughtful of him.

ROB: My dad was the sixth Beatle.

TOM: The sixth? I don't think there were ever six of them.

ROB: It was short lived. As I say too much talent in my family, makes others feel bad.

TOM: Of course.

ROB: My musical talents tend to draw in the girls too. Have you got a girlfriend?

TOM: No not at the moment.

ROB: The girls from home won't leave me alone; I get messages all the time. They go crazy for a musician.

TOM: Crazy! So you have a girlfriend?

ROB: Well they're more like fans really.

TOM: Fans, of course. Shall I show you the cafeteria?

ROB: Sure. We had a restaurant at my old school, run by top chefs.

TOM: One of which was your dad?

ROB: No don't be daft he has people to cook for him, he doesn't cook himself.

TOM: Of course he doesn't. I'm just wondering if you're so rich why you've moved to our very working class village and our very average school.

ROB: An experiment.

TOM: An experiment?

ROB: Yes. Why else would I be here? I'm seeing how the other half live. I know what your suspicious mind is thinking. My parents are still together you know, they haven't separated. My dad didn't have an affair with his personal assistant. We haven't had to sell our mansion, we still have a big house in London with a Jacuzzi and cinema room. I still get fan mail from local girls. My thousands of friends are lost without me. I'm still officially registered in the top school in the country which I will return to after this experiment is over. And my dad is still a travelling author who advises the Prime Minister and socialises with the Beckhams.

TOM: Good story, Rob, it just needs more dragons. This isn't such a bad school; you'll like it here. Come on, I'll show you where your form room is.

Task:

What is the common theme in these two scenes? In pairs, improvise a scene where you are both trying to outdo one another.

Example:

A: My mum is a better driver than your mum.

B: Well my dad can run faster than your dad.

A: Well my gran is better at hopscotch than your gran.

B: Well my dog can bark louder than your dog.

A: Well my cat can sing the EastEnders theme tune better than your cat.

B: Well my hamster can recite Shakespeare better than your hamster.

Continue...

Performers can get more bizarre with their statements until one performer can't think of anything to outdo the other, at which point that performer says, 'You win!'

Task:

Choose a script to work on. Because of the level of exaggeration in some of the characters' dialogue it would be useful at this point to think about vocal expression. Highlight key words which require more vocal emphasis.

Facial expression is important to show the doubt in the characters of Joe and Tom. Try performing it in different ways:

    a. With their doubt clear from the outset.

    b. With their doubt appearing to the audience gradually.

    c. With their doubt only becoming clear towards then end.

Which works best from an audience's perspective?

Task:

Try *The Piano Exam* stood up, then sat down. Which is more effective? Or is it more effective to have one seated and one standing? Does this help to demonstrate status? Is there a shift in stage status? How could this be portrayed?

Try establishing which stage areas will be used for *More Dragons*. Could each area have one symbolic prop to represent the room? For example, a book for the library, or a guitar for the music room. Try it with and without props. Do the props give the characters something to physically do in each room? Is this more effective than minimalist staging?

The scenes would need staging very differently. *The Piano Exam* is more static, and *More Dragons* uses all areas of the stage. Although projections could be used to represent each area of the school.

Trouble in the Enchanted Forest

FAIRY: Morning, Pixie, Elf. I have to speak to you both about something.

ELF: If it's about the attack on the east side of the enchanted forest-

PIXIE: We know!

FAIRY: So, what shall we do about it?

ELF: We don't even know what's causing the trees to fall.

PIXIE: I think it's a big, ugly monstrous giant who is coming to gobble us all up!

ELF/FAIRY: Pixie!!

PIXIE: Well what else could it be?

FAIRY: I heard a rumble like thunder last night and when I peeked out of the window another tree had fallen.

ELF: I think we should hide in the bushes this afternoon and see for ourselves.

PIXIE: You will have to take that silly crown off, Fairy. If that catches the light we'll be sure to get caught, then we will be the first to get eaten by the giant!

FAIRY: First of all, this crown is elegant not silly! Second of all there is NO GIANT!

(Later that day, in the bushes...)

ELF: Pixie, will you keep still? You're going to give us away.

PIXIE: This is a prickly bush!

FAIRY: Look, look at that it's a, it's a...

ELF: It's a giant!

PIXIE: Told you!

ELF: A giant with a ginormous metal arm, and teeth.

PIXIE: Run for your lives!

FAIRY: Am I the bravest here? *(She stands and shouts)* Hey, you! Leave our forest alone, you big bully.

ELF: She's cracked!

PIXIE: She's going to be his starter!

ELF: I'm a little concerned about his main meal and dessert! I'm with you Pixie...RUN!

Task:

A good activity for younger performers would be to create a set for this scene. For example, using green, brown and red paint to create a huge tree, or making leaves out of the performers handprints to create the bush the characters hide in.

Performers could write a short monologue to portray the character's feelings about the destruction of their environment which could be inserted into the scene.

This could lead to other creative work based on the theme of the environment and climate change. The following monologue could be used to further discuss the effects of climate change with younger children.

Alfie

Suitability: Pre-teen
Character: Ben/Betsie

*(**BEN/BETSIE** is looking forward to Christmas time and wintery weather as he/she gets to spend time with someone special.)*

BEN/BETSIE: I know we only have a short time together, Alfie, but I want you to know that you are amazing, and even though you are deteriorating every day you remain the same to me. I love getting up and seeing your big smile out of my bedroom window, but my mum says you will be gone soon and I should prepare myself. That makes me sad, but I'm hoping you will be back next year. Christmas just isn't the same without you. I'm going to buy you a new bobble hat with a matching scarf, I think red would suit you best. Oh no, Alfie, you've lost an eye, I hope that wasn't painful. I bet that pesky dog next door had something to do with it. Mum always says, 'She's just being playful, she's only a puppy,' like losing an eye isn't serious! And what is that yellow streak down your left side? Oh my goodness that just isn't cool, and it is certainly not being playful! It's sabotage!

Sometimes I feel like we only have each other, Alfie. You're the only one who listens to me and I know how much you enjoy our days in the snow. I don't want the sun to come back, I can't bear to see you disappear for another year. Becoming a puddle is all you have to look forward to and I bet that dog next door will just love paddling in you, or worse. That animal has no respect.

You may be shrinking in front of my very eyes but my love for you is greater than ever. I am praying for a big freeze next winter so we can be together again, and I promise you this, Alfie, I will build the biggest animal proof barricade all the way around you. Playful puppy? I don't think so, more like devil dog! Happy New Year, Alfie, see you again next year.

(*Aside.*) I think I'd better save the global warming chat for another time.

Mission Complete

JOHNNY: They're after me, don't turn around just keep going. Sharp left, sharp left! Slow down, okay take a sharp right and three, two, one, jump. Luke, you're supposed to be on my side. Get the baddies, you're going to get us obliterated. Hi, Jack101 join us, we need to get the crystal, Luke keeps forgetting whose side he's on. Right, Jack, you take the lead and pick up any weapons you find on the way.

MUM: Johnny, your tea's ready.

JOHNNY: I'll be down in a minute.

MUM: Now, Johnny.

JOHNNY: Please, Mum just five more minutes. I need to defeat the Power Lord.

MUM: Your tea is going cold.

JOHNNY: I'll microwave it.

MUM: Now, Johnny!

JOHNNY: Ok, I'm coming. Sorry, lads, I've got to go. I'll be back later. Don't get us killed. Mum, do you have to be like that when I'm online with my friends? They can hear everything you say, you know.

MUM: It's not good for you, being on that machine all day. You need fresh air like I got as a kid. We would play out all day until our parents called us in for tea. We didn't have phones, video games or gadgets.

JOHNNY: So what did you have?

MUM: We had imagination and a whole lot of fun.

JOHNNY: I don't see how you can have fun with nothing but your imagination. The seventies sound boring.

MUM: It was magical and expanded the mind more than that games console ever could.

JOHNNY: Fine, I'll go out and play. I'll be back in a few hours or when boredom takes over me.

MUM: Good.

JOHNNY: Ok I'm going out to play then, without gadgets. You know, in the fresh air with my imagination. I won't take my phone with me because that might stunt my creativity when playing my new imagination-fuelled games. I'll just leave it on the side here. Like you said before, it's just as safe now as it was back then, things are just reported more.

MUM: Are you testing me?

JOHNNY: No, Mum, but you didn't need a phone for emergencies, so I'll be fine too. Besides I can run fast if faced with danger.

MUM: Why don't you call for your friends?

JOHNNY: Sure I'll go and *call* for them. What exactly does that mean? Is it seventies speak for knock on their front door?

MUM: No one calls for anyone these days, it's such a shame.

JOHNNY: Okay, Mum, so I'm going now, out on my own. Bye then.

MUM: Wait!

JOHNNY: I knew it. You're worried. You're having second thoughts.

MUM: You forgot your coat.

JOHNNY: Oh. I didn't see that coming. Well, off I go into the unknown, it's getting a bit dark though. Mum, are you sure you're ok with this? You can always let me back online and keep an eye on me.

MUM: Bye, son, zip your coat up.

JOHNNY: Ok I'm leaving now, off I go down the drive and on to the streets, where it's getting a bit dark, and there are a few strangers about.

MUM: Fine! You win. You can have twenty more minutes gaming. But then it's going off.

JOHNNY: Deal. Hey guys, this is Johnny reporting back. Sorry it took so long, there was more than one operation I needed to complete today. Let's just say mission accomplished.

Task:

This duologue could lead into an exploration of childhood through the decades. Each group is given a different decade to research then create a collage or spider diagram of key childhood pastimes during that period. Each group attempts to justify why growing up in their given era was most fulfilling.

Each group creates a tableau that sums up childhood in that decade. The class forms a timeline using the tableaus across the space.

What might the parent's anxieties be and how may they differ from decade to decade? Choose one or two confident performers to step out of the timeline to express the parents' feelings in character. Alternatively, create a thought tunnel; this is where the performers form a human tunnel by standing in two lines. The teacher walks down the centre in character as the performers call out the thoughts in the characters head as they pass through the tunnel.

Now think about a modern-day child being transported back in time. Repeat the thought tunnel exercise for each decade, what would a child from today think about childhood in each decade.

Using these thoughts create a scene where a modern-day child goes back in time to meet children from a previous decade.

Using the duologue as a stimulus, devise a scene where:

> a. Johnny goes back in time and meets his mum as a child in the seventies.
>
> b. Mum is a child and we see how she related to her parents.

Use physicality to show how involved Johnny is when he is playing on his games console.

Add some asides to the audience to get a deeper insight into how Johnny and his mum are feeling.

Monologues could be written to allow the actor to think about the character's inner thoughts. This could be followed up by a hot seating exercise.

Who Needs Enemies

The following extract is from a short play called *Who Needs Enemies*, which has since been developed into a full-length play and is more appropriate for older teen performers.

*(**CLAIRE** is sat reading a book in her night clothes. There is a loud knock at the door which startles her. The knock becomes a heavy rap and **CLAIRE** walks warily towards the door.)*

DEE: Claire, let me in, I know you're there.

(More desperate knocking.)

DEE: Answer the flaming door, Claire.

*(**CLAIRE** opens the door to see **DEE** stood with blood smeared down her top and on her hands.)*

CLAIRE: Dee, what the hell's wrong?

(Looking her up and down.)

CLAIRE: Jesus Christ what happened to you? Are you ok? Get in here, come in.

*(**CLAIRE** shows her in and signals for her to sit down, quickly grabbing a towel with selfish concern for the sofa. **CLAIRE** kneels in front of **DEE**.)*

CLAIRE: Are you hurt?

*(**DEE** is shaking and barely able to speak.)*

DEE: I...

CLAIRE: Did someone do this to you?

DEE: I'm not hurt, I just banged my head.

CLAIRE: How?

DEE: An accident.

CLAIRE: What sort of accident?

*(**CLAIRE** goes to the window and pulls back the curtain.)*

CLAIRE: How the hell have you managed to drive that? Are you sure you're not hurt? I'm going to ring an ambulance to be sure.

DEE: No!

CLAIRE: Why? Dee don't be ridiculous you're hurt.

DEE: I'm fine, you can't ring an ambulance.

CLAIRE: Then tell me why not.

DEE: I don't want a flaming ambulance!

CLAIRE: OK. For God's sake calm down. Look, you're shaking.

*(**CLAIRE** fetches **DEE** a glass of water.)*

CLAIRE: Please tell me what's going on, what happened to you tonight?

*(**DEE** takes a sip of water.)*

CLAIRE: Please, Dee, tell me. In your own time.

*(**DEE** glances briefly at **CLAIRE** then stares at the floor. Both sit in silence, briefly. **CLAIRE** reaches for **DEE**'s glass and starts to drink. **DEE** gets up and begins to pace the room. The silence continues, **CLAIRE** watches as **DEE** paces more frantically. She grabs **DEE**'s arm.)*

CLAIRE: Stop! For God's sake, stop!

*(**DEE** looks **CLAIRE** in the eye, then glances at the photos on the mantelpiece.)*

DEE: You're so lucky.

*(She picks up a photo of **CLAIRE** on her wedding day.)*

DEE: I've always been in the background, haven't I? Even when we were kids, it was you that won the competitions. You who decided what games we'd play. You that got picked for all the teams first and had to persuade the captain to take me on. You who went to uni. You who had a great job, great future, great boyfriend, always you! I was like your pathetic little shadow, I still am.

CLAIRE: Are you angry with me?

DEE: No.

CLAIRE: Dee, I've never thought you were in my shadow. You're my best mate you always have been. You could never change that.

DEE: You don't know me as well as you think.

CLAIRE: Will you please just tell me what went on tonight? Why are you acting so strangely?

And where did the blood come from if it's not yours?

(A long silence.)

CLAIRE: Dee, you need to tell me what the hell is going on. I'm starting to get pissed off, and I will ring the police.

DEE: You're pissed off? Jesus, Claire, it's always about you, about how you feel. Everything is on your terms.

CLAIRE: Just tell me!

*(**DEE** puts her head in her hands. After a short silence **DEE** looks up, she is crying.)*

DEE: It wasn't my fault, I swerved to avoid a rabbit, lost control. I didn't see it coming.

CLAIRE: See what? Another car?

DEE: Yes. I didn't see it, I'm sorry. It's not my fault.

CLAIRE: Look, the police obviously don't think it's your fault if they let you go.

DEE: I didn't phone the police. Claire, you're going to kill me. I've had a drink.

CLAIRE: How bloody stupid can you be?

DEE: I know, but I only had a mile to go, I thought I'd be ok.

*(**CLAIRE** reaches for the phone.)*

DEE: Please, Claire don't do this.

CLAIRE: What if someone's hurt?

DEE: They're not!

CLAIRE: How can you be sure?

*(**DEE** jumps up and hastily grabs the phone.)*

DEE: Please.

CLAIRE: How can you be sure they're not hurt? You left the scene of the accident.

DEE: I'm sure.

CLAIRE: How can you be?

DEE: Stop it, ok? I'm sure.

CLAIRE: How?

DEE: Because...

CLAIRE: Because what?!

DEE: Because he's dead, ok? He's dead!

*(**CLAIRE**, in shock, returns slowly to the sofa.)*

CLAIRE: Jesus Christ!

DEE: It wasn't my fault.

CLAIRE: It never is.

DEE: I didn't see it coming.

CLAIRE: You were drunk!

(Pause.)

CLAIRE: You killed someone and left them, just bloody left them!

DEE: I didn't mean to.

CLAIRE: What, kill them or leave them? You are unbelievable. Where did the blood come from? It's not just from you, Dee, tell me where the damn blood came from!

DEE: I checked the body.

CLAIRE: For what? Money? Did you rob him?

DEE: For a pulse, Claire, a pulse.

CLAIRE: Then you left? You just got up and left the poor sod to rot?

DEE: No! Not exactly.

CLAIRE: What do you mean?

DEE: I need your help, Claire. You have to help me.

CLAIRE: I have spent my whole life helping you, digging you out of situations, but you've overstepped the mark this time. We need to ring the police, explain you were scared, tell them you're sorry for leaving the scene and take your punishment. You need to tell them where the other car and the body is.

DEE: I can't.

CLAIRE: Yes, you can. You have to. They'll catch up with you eventually and the consequences will be worse.

DEE: You don't understand.

CLAIRE: You're right there.

DEE: You don't understand, I can't tell them where the body is.

CLAIRE: Why?

(Beat.)

CLAIRE: Why?

(Beat.)

CLAIRE: Jesus Christ, why can't you tell them where the body is?

DEE: Because it's in my car!

CLAIRE: What?

DEE: I somehow managed to get him in the boot.

CLAIRE: The boot! You're not a flaming gangster, Dee! You idiot!

DEE: I know, I'm sorry.

CLAIRE: Sorry doesn't even begin to cover it.

DEE: I'm sorry.

CLAIRE: I know, you said. Now let me think.

*(**CLAIRE** goes to the window and takes another look at the car.)*

CLAIRE: We have to tell the police.

DEE: No, please.

CLAIRE: What choice have you got?

DEE: You could help me.

CLAIRE: Help you what?

DEE: Get rid of him.

CLAIRE: You're insane. No, Dee, I can't get involved. Besides, he will have a family. A wife, children, parents; they deserve to know.

DEE: I'll go to prison.

CLAIRE: You don't know that.

DEE: I moved the body; they're going to wonder why.

CLAIRE: I wonder why, Dee! You stupid, stupid woman.

DEE: Ok I get it, but I've done it now so please just help me. No one will ever find out. We can get away with this.

CLAIRE: And spend the rest of our lives regretting it, feeling guilty.

DEE: What about the guilt you'll feel if you don't help me!

CLAIRE: You selfish cow! You come to my house in the middle of the night, having committed a hit and run, and you dare to try and guilt trip me.

DEE: I know, I'm sorry. But, Claire, I'm desperate.

CLAIRE: I can't risk this. Think what it would do to Steve if he found out.

DEE: You owe me!

CLAIRE: Don't start. That was years ago, you hardly knew him.

DEE: You stole him.

CLAIRE: You're bitter and twisted.

DEE: I was your best friend, best friends don't do things like that.

CLAIRE: Grow up and move on.

DEE: Help me move on. I need your help, please.

Task:

There are hints in the script to their issues in the past. Devise a series of flashbacks to create a backstory for the characters.

Devise flash forwards. Does Claire help Dee and if so, in what way?

The play ends with a dramatic twist. Consider what that twist might be. Devise the final scene of *Who Needs Enemies*.

There are moments of tension between the characters, consider proxemics when staging it (the positioning between characters). At what moment would they get closer to one another? Annotate the script with arrows to show when the characters move closer, and when they move apart.

< > Move apart > < Move closer

How would the levels of tension appear on a tension graph?

Use of pause would need to be considered to highlight their tension and frustration. An elongated moment of silence would be effective, decide where this moment should be. What might the characters do physically at this point? Remain still? Pace around the room? Show agitation? Glances towards each other? Eye contact or avoiding eye contact?

Voice – Think about dynamics. Try performing the scene without raising voices, then again with rising vocals. Which creates more tension?

Working with an Ensemble Play

The following extract is from *Intrusion*, a play about mental health. In particular OCD and intrusive thoughts.

Extract One

(A minimalistic set. Perhaps a few black chairs/stools scattered around the stage. The dialogue which is not allocated to a specific character can be delivered chorally or by individual members of the ensemble.)

Ordinary, that's how life starts,

Just ordinary.

A blank canvas.

So what triggers change from ordinary to extraordinary?

SUSAN: That is my mother. She's kind, gentle and perfectly normal in every way, although not in a boring way. I'm not saying she isn't extraordinary; she is. She's my mum and would do anything for me. But I love the fact that she's normal, predictable and always there. She makes me feel safe when external things don't. She doesn't recognise my secret. It hasn't occurred to her that I think differently to other kids. I wear the mask well. This is my father; he is strong, brave and unassuming. He doesn't realise how much my mum does for him. She has been his rock for so long that it has become normal. Normal, what does that even mean? We are an ordinary family, in an ordinary street, in an extraordinary world.

So why didn't she feel normal deep inside?

Even bedtime didn't give her relief, sleep didn't come easily to Susan.

Tossing, turning, floating, dreaming, waking, night terrors.

She wakes.

Her teddy falls to the floor.

She reaches for it.

And holds him tight.

Morning, Orange Ted.

She meticulously makes the bed.

The birds sing.

The sun shines.

Susan opens the curtains.

Right then left.

It's bright.

She feels the heat on her face.

The sun intrudes on her space.

Intrusion, part of her every waking moment.

What if that intruder is you?

She wasn't helpless. She didn't need anyone's help, at least that's what she believed.

SUSAN: I can control it myself.

She repeated this to herself, over and over. Eight times a day to be precise. She told herself this over and over, eight times a day to be precise. Part of her morning ritual.

I can control you.
I can control you.
I can control you.
I can control you.
I can control you.
I can control you.
I can control you
I *can* control you.
I can control me.

She lied. She felt like she was being watched. Like a stalker's victim. Following her slowly, her every step, her every move, wherever she went. An intruder impinging on her life, day in day out, night after night. The intruder was never far away but what if that intruder turned out to be you?

She had no idea when it first started, no memory of the first attack, the first image. It had just always been there. Neither parent noticed. She kept her secret well-hidden and the intruder deep inside her mind.

Task:

Place approximately eight chairs on stage. Play instrumental music and ask the group to choreograph an opening sequence to create some starting positions.

Leave the music playing and choreograph some gestures in unison to go with the first five lines of dialogue. Decide if they are spoken by individuals or chorally. They could also be repeated or echoed.

Create tableaus to illustrate Susan's speech about her family.

The 'sleep' section would benefit from music or creating a soundscape. Experiment with vocal dynamics on the line:

Tossing, turning, floating, dreaming, waking, night terrors.

Perhaps repeating the line several times, allowing voices to get louder. Physically show Susan's discomfort at night with a carefully choreographed sequence. Then change the pace as she snaps into reality and wakes.

Use the 'I can control you' lines to experiment with different ways of delivering the line. Emphasising different words in the sentence and using a variety of dynamics whilst experimenting with proxemics. For example, physically closing in on Susan's character.

The final section of dialogue could be delivered as a chorus using unison to portray the movement.

There are limitless ways to perform an ensemble piece, so these are only suggestions.

The following extracts come from different moments in the play and depict Susan at different ages. Perhaps give small groups a different piece each to experiment with. Some of these extracts use stichomythic dialogue and are extremely fast-paced as the lines bounce off of each other.

Extract Two

Susan Jameson is seven years old.

Quiet child.

Ssh.

One might imagine she would be an odd child.

One would be wrong.

Susan was quiet, unassuming, but perfectly normal.

SUSAN: Look at this, Joe, someone has moved my shoes. They should be in a straight line directly under my window sill, was it you? No, Joe, you're doing it wrong, the right should be in front of the left by two finger spaces. Use your finger. You're so stupid.

Susan didn't have many friends; it wasn't anything to do with her secret, because no one but Joe knew about it. She kept the disguise well.

SUSAN: Joe you can go now I have something I need to do.

She liked to be alone.

SUSAN: Mr Ted, you go next to Nellie and I'll tie you to Orange Ted. And if I wrap this ribbon around Sooty, Sweep and Sue you will be all tied together.

Bound together.

But this wasn't some sick game.

Susan feared.

Feared pretty much everything.

And if there was a fire.

Susan wanted to save all her toys.

It wouldn't be fair to save one.

It wasn't strange behaviour.

It was logical.

Wasn't it?

SUSAN: Now, Orange Ted, you're in charge! If I tie you all to my bean bag, then if I have to throw you out of the window you will land softly.

She planned the escape.

She would jump last and they would catch her.

Intrusion.

Intrusion alert.

Sizzle.

    Crack.

        Pop.

            Sizzle.

                Crack.

                Pop.

                Fire!

I can't breathe.

I can't breathe.

Choking.

    Help me.

        Evacuate.

            Jump.

                Splat.

                Blood.

Pain.

Death!

Shake it off.

Reality.

Susan was perfectly normal.

Normal, usual, standard, typical, stock, common, ordinary, sane.

At least on the outside, no one would suspect her inner turmoil, her disturbances that stopped her in her tracks.

The confusion she felt, she did not share.

If she did, maybe her parents would not love her.

SUSAN: Or worse they won't believe me.

Extract Three

Eight is a safe,

Safe,

Number, she thought,

And so it was that the number eight became a safe haven.

It protected her from evil.

It kept Susan safe.

'Susan,' said Mrs O'Keefe.

SUSAN: Yes, Miss?

MRS O'KEEFE: Why haven't you answered number six?

SUSAN: It was too hard, Miss.

MRS O'KEEFE: It gets progressively harder, Susan, and you've answered number ten, and you've missed out number nine as well.

SUSAN: Sorry.

MRS O'KEEFE: Six times six, Susan.

SUSAN: I can't remember.

MELISSA: (*Raises hand.*) Ooh, ooh, ooh. I know it, I know it.

MRS O'KEEFE: You know the answer, we've been doing the six times tables for weeks.

MELISSA: Me, Miss. Me, Miss.

MRS O'KEEFE: Yes, Melissa.

MELISSA: It's thirty-six, Miss.

MRS O'KEEFE: Thank you, Melissa.

(*The ensemble recites the six times table.*)

One times six is?

MELISSA: Six.

Six, six, six.

Two times six is?

SUSAN: Twelve

Three times six, six, six, six, six.

Intrusion.

She pulled out a knife almost matching the size of her small frame.

And she thrust it into her teacher's back.

MRS O'KEEFE: Susan, are you listening to me?

SUSAN: Miss, I feel unwell may I be excused?

Joe, Joe, Joe!

SUSAN: Joe, where are you?

JOE: Six, six, six.

Six, six, six.

SUSAN: Why would you say that, Joe?

He teased.

Stop! She yelled..

JOE: Six, six, six.

SUSAN: Stop! Joe, stop!

He didn't stop.

She cried.

He laughed.

Extract Four

SUSAN: I was only a teenager when mother died.

Susan felt angry.

Susan felt lost.

Her anxiety levels increased.

Susan was alone.

Classroom 2.30.

Teacher.

Pupils.

Tension.

    Tick.

Tick.

Tick.

Tock.

Tap.

Tap.

Test.

Breathe.

Test.

Breathe.

Yawn.

She rubs her eyes.

Inhale.

Exhale.

Daydream.

Watch the clock.

Heads up.

Face me.

Tap.

Tap.

Tap.

Heads down.

Write.

Daydream.

Wanting to be elsewhere.

Yawn.

Tick tick tock.

Inhale.

Exhale.

2.45.

15 minutes.

Weekend.

      Friends.

         Tap.

         Tap.

           Write.

              Think.

              Yawn.

Daydream.

Tick.

  Tick.

      Tick tock tick tock tick tock.

Watch.

Time.

Watch the clock.

Pace.

  Pace.

Pace.

Shoes clonking.

Annoying.

Frustrating.

Think.

Can't think.

Inhale.

Exhale.

Think.

Can't.

Think harder!

Find answer.

No answer.

Wrong answer.

Giving up.

Yawn.

Pace.

Monotony.

Pace.

Repeat.

Pace.

Retreat.

Teacher retreat!

She doesn't.

Extract Five

Into the driver's seat he goes.

He can take his ale.

ADDY: I can take my drink.

Keys.

    Ignition.

        Nothing.

           Try again.

                Ignition.

                    Nothing.

                        Sigh.

                            Ignition.

                                Revs.

                                    Revs harder.

                                        Show off.

                                          Accelerator.

She wants to get out.

But.

But…

SUSAN: Words fail me.

No going back.

My seat belt clicks.

No other clicks.

Engine revs.

The trees surround us.

Flashing by.

Fast.

  So fast.

    Slow down.

        Laugh.

          They laugh.

SUSAN: I'm not laughing.

Chill out!

Noise of their laughs ringing through her ears.

Skid.

  Brake.

    Slow motion.

But in reality, the car spins fast.

Tree.

  Too late.

    Silence.

      Deathly silence.

But there was only one click.

SUSAN: My click.

She's disorientated.

        Silence.

        Silence.

SUSAN: Only my panic.

She looks around.

SUSAN: There's just me. Still in my seat.

Blood.

Blood on her face.

But silence.

It's haunting.

SUSAN: Are you ok?

My words ring through the pain in my head.

Silence.

SUSAN: Are you all OK?

Panic builds.

Fumbling for the seat belt.

SUSAN: I need to get out.

Click.

Silence.

SUSAN: Please, someone help. Are you all OK?

Deathly silence.

Death.

Only silence.

Shake it off.

TERRY: Chill out, Suzy! We're only going for a spin.

Stichomythic Dialogue

Ensemble Work

Performers can experiment with the three short stand-alone ensemble scenes below. They are written using stichomythic dialogue therefore in delivery, pace is important. There are deliberately no character names so that performers can experiment with the delivery in an ensemble style. An example would be to use choral speaking, echoing of lines, varying vocal dynamics and repetition. Music and choreographed movement is encouraged as is the use of canon and unison.

Extract One

Life Changing Moment

- Hope
- Fingers crossed
- Four-leaf clover
- Rabbit's foot
- Ewww
- Good luck to me
- Could be life changing
- Life changing
- Anticipation
- My heart's racing
- D-dum, d-dum, d-dum
- Beating faster
- Here we go
- This is it
- My life changing moment
- Ball number twenty-five
- Check
- Ball number four

- Check
- Ball number thirty-five
- Oh my days!
- Check, check, check
- Check again
- Check
- Ball number forty-three
- I can hardly believe this
- Believe it
- Ball number eleven
- Check
- Heart racing, pounding, beating out of my chest
- Cross everything
- Everything crossed
- I missed it, oh my days! I missed it. What did they say?
- Rewind! REWIND!!
- Ball number fourteen
- Did they say fourteen?
- Fourteen
- Fourteen!
- Time freezes!
- Slow motion takes over
- We celebrate
- Life changing
- Hello, I think I may have just won the jackpot
- Twenty-five, four, thirty-five, forty-three, eleven, fourteen
- Holy shhh-
- Shall we? (*Leads centre stage.*)
- A dozen roses
- As requested
- The finest diamonds
- As demanded
- Three-course meal madam/sir
- A new woman/man

- A changed person
- A person with so much more, yet so little
- Friends turn their backs
- Who cares, I have more, more than you, and you
- Yet she/he has so much less
- Family feuds
- You gave her more than me, it's not fair
- I deserve more, I'm your sister
- The ladies/fellas love me
- They love your bank balance
- I'm loved
- Superficially
- I'm important
- I'm leaving you
- You're lonely
- I have everything
- You have nothing but heartache ahead
- You've changed

Extract Two

Distorted Reality

- Cyber-reality
- Happy family, happy relationships, happy life
- My friends are the best
- My social life is hectic
- Loving life
- Hashtag this
- Hashtag that
- Look at me
- Like me
- Selfie

- Like
- Pout
- Selfie
- More likes
- Popular
- Self-worth

- Reality
- She sat with her hands over her ears
- The shouting got louder
- 'Get up. You pathetic woman'
- Please stop
- 'Why do you need to be so aggressive?'
- 'You make me, it's your fault I'm like this'
- More shouting
- It's as if I don't exist
- They scream and yell until
- Mum cries
- Then he is sorry

- Cyber-life
- Having a night in with the family
- Hashtag family time
- Lies
- Fake news
- Her news was fake, or at least distorted because the truth didn't ooze perfection
- Perfection
- Perfection at the touch of a button
- Post
- Camouflaging reality
- Because it's what you do
- Because it hurts less

- Reality
- Lonely

- Four walls of the bedroom
- Like a cell I can't escape
- Homework
- More homework
- School stress
- It's about grades, grades, grades
- It's about being top of the class
- Hitting targets
- Achievement
- When did it stop being ok to be average? When did it stop being ok to fail? We can learn from failure, can't we?
- Strive harder
- Strive for success
- Strive for perfection
- Be perfect or be insignificant

- Cyber-school
- Google
- Search the answers
- Copy and paste
- Don't need to think for myself, can't think anymore
- I don't want to risk being wrong, so I turn to the all- knowing one
- Alexa
- Alexa knows
- Alexa knows everything

- Everything...the truth
- My truth
- My truth is that I don't exist in the real world
- No one understands me, no one is interested in me, no real friends
- Nothing is about me

- Online, I'm in control of me
- Selfie
- You're so pretty
- Says you

- You're beaut-
- Says you
- Mutual admiration
- Fake friends
- Hundreds of friends
- Admirers
- Ego boosting likes
- Until...
- The cyberworld turns on you...

Extract Three

Eat

- Breakfast time!
- I'm not hungry, Mum
- Eat or you won't have any energy
- I'm fine, honest
- You need to eat, there's nothing on you
- I'll have an apple
- Mum; too exhausted from days, weeks, months of the same argument
- Doesn't argue
- One apple
- Bite
- Crunch
- Chew
- Chewing feels endless
- Reluctance as she swallows
- Gag reflex
- Bin
- School
- Friends

- Invite to a party!
- Panic
- Chocolate cake
- Crisps
- Pop
- Birthday cake
- Sausage on sticks
- Pop
- Cream Cake
- Ice cream
- Carrot cake
- Carrot cake
- Cake
- Carrots plural
- Carrot singular
- A single carrot
- A bite
- Just one bite
- Just one bite of the carrot
- Bite
- Chew
- It's just a carrot
- Chocolate fountain!!
- Avoid
- Watch but don't touch
- Guilty pleasures
- No pleasure
- Satisfaction from denying myself
- Denial
- I am healthy
- I don't like sweets
- I don't eat sweets
- I can't eat sweets
- Party bag

- Fake smile
- Accept the bag
- Bin the bag
- Too much sugar, they said
- Unhealthy
- Dr Sparks looked at me, Dr Sparks weighed me, Dr Sparks accused me of being unhealthy
- She said what I'm doing to myself is unhealthy
- Mum looked on with sadness in her eyes
- If only they'd understand
- Mirrors, Mirrors everywhere
- Don't like to look but feeling compelled
- I look fat
- If only they could understand
- Exercise regime
- Sit ups, one hundred
- Push harder
- Work harder
- Press ups, one hundred
- Don't give up
- Squats…as many as I can till I can't feel my legs
- Lunch time!
- No thanks, Mum
- I'm still full from breakfast
- You need to eat
- You must eat
- You will die if you carry on
- Here we go cue the anorexic pictures
- Shock tactics
- But, Mum that won't be me
- I do eat
- Enough to feed a toddler
- I don't want to be a fat dancer
- You won't be a dancer at all if you're dead

- Shock tactics
- Momentary effect
- Then forgotten
- I've made you a sandwich
- Nibble
- Slowly
- Nibble
- Chew endlessly
- Swallow reluctantly
- Family indulging around me
- Over indulgence
- Thirty minutes later
- The final nibble
- Straight upstairs
- Exercise quietly
- Letter box
- Letters drop
- Letter for the guardian of
- Of
- Of me
- And so the process started
- CAMHS they call it
- Children's mental health
- I'm normal
- I just don't like sweets
- Or fat
- Or carbohydrates
- Or protein
- Or…or…
- FOOD!
- Visit the fridge, stare for a while
- Resist
- Close the fridge
- Dad's sad eyes, Mum's sad eyes

- Desperate, lost, no longer have an answer
- Teatime!
- I'll make tea for you all
- She liked to cook
- To feed others
- Was she tempted to eat what she cooked?
- She would try it and entertain the smallest portion
- But no meat, not anymore
- Vegetarianism
- Making meals more difficult to think of
- So she cooked
- We sat as a family
- And watched her pick
- Frustrating
- Meal times were not happy in the Chorley household.
- Food dominated every thought in this family
- Every argument
- It was difficult to attend any social occasions
- Food brought misery
- Depression
- Mental health nurse
- Session one
- What do you like about yourself, Jess?
- I don't know
- What do you think others like about you?
- Nothing
- Nothing?
- Are you kind?
- Generous?
- A good friend?
- I think so
- What makes you happy?
- Dancing

The scenes can end there or can be extended by the performers as a classroom activity and developed into a devised piece. Naturalistic scenes could be devised using the themes in the script.

Exploring Character

The following extract is from the play *It Started with a Kidnap*. The play is very character based and is set in a local amateur dramatics society.

ADAM: The show must go on. So let's crack on with our first audition.

MIRIAM: Mildred, why don't you go first, show these young ones how it's done.

MILDRED: I'd be honoured, Miriam. Where do you want me?

ADAM: Centre stage, Mavis.

ALL: Mildred.

MILDRED: Really, Adam? It's been a year. Okay, here we go, I'm going to portray the detective.

MIRIAM: You can't.

MILDRED: Why not?

MIRIAM: The character is a man.

MILDRED: Why?

MIRIAM: Because, Mildred, that is how the part is written. I was going with a Sherlock kind of feel.

JULIE: I really think we should move with the times, Miriam.

MIRIAM: Did you write it, Julie? Did you? Do you know how long this took me? If I wanted a Miss Marple vibe, I would have written it that way.

SUE: Just saying, but we only have two males in the company, and Jack is the stiff.

JACK: I'm stiff.

ADAM: Then it's settled then. I'll play the lead and *I will* portray the character as the playwright intended.

MIRIAM: Thank you. Read for the part of Mrs Crosney, Mildred.

MILDRED: But I don't want to play Mrs Crosney. She doesn't come into it until act two, and we all know there'll be no one watching by then.

MIRIAM: Fine, let's do the auditions as a workshop. Everyone stand.

JULIE: I think we should warm up.

SUE: Just crack on, we have Adam's mystery meeting this evening.

MIRIAM: Fine. Everyone; massage your face.

SUE: Really?

MIRIAM: And hum. You don't need to massage at the same time.

JACK: I'm up for a massage.

SUE: I bet you are, Jack.

JACK: Jen?

JEN: No, Jack.

MIRIAM: Stay on task lovelies. Now "Ah" hold it, hold the note. Fiona, I can't hear you, love. "Te" hold for four and "Do-Re-Mi" and relax.

SUE: This must be how the von Trapp kids felt.

MIRIAM: And shake out the whole body, right from your fingertips to your toes. Now I will say a line from the play, and you will each deliver it in turn. Okay, lovelies, let's do this.

ANDREA: Excuse me, I don't feel comfortable speaking in front of everyone.

HELENA: But that's why you're here, to build confidence and enhance that rather poor excuse for a CV.

ANDREA: But I just don't feel comfortable in public, and definitely not on stage.

HELENA: Of course you do. The theatre is in your blood.

ANDREA: I'm good with props.

MIRIAM: Just try your best, you might surprise yourself. Okay, so your line is, "Oh no, I can't believe it. I think he's dead!" And I want facial expression, intonation and expressive body language. Julie, you're first.

*(They each repeat the line, with a lack of enthusiasm or talent. **JULIE** does a few breathing exercises before delivering the lines, **MIA** just seems distracted. Sue has a sarcastic tone, **JEN** has a flirty undertone. **JACK** is wooden and gets the words wrong, **HELENA** is overconfident. **ANDREA** has no expression at all, **MILDRED** over emphasises words. **FIONA** is so quiet they all step towards her to hear. **ADAM** sits at the side drinking from a hip flask, getting gradually more intoxicated.)*

JULIE: *(She starts with some deep breathing.)* Okay, I'm ready now, I'm in the moment, "Oh no, I can't believe it. I think he's dead!"

MIRIAM: Mia.

MIA: "Oh no, I can't believe it I think he's…" Sorry what was the line again?

ADAM: Dead, I think he's dead!

MIRIAM: Never mind. Sue, you're up.

SUE: "Oh no, I can't believe it. I think he's dead!"

MIRIAM: Could you maybe take it a bit more seriously, maybe add panic to your voice.

SUE: I'll give it a miss.

MIRIAM: Fine. Jen you go.

JEN: "Oh no, I can't believe it. I think he's dead!"

MIRIAM: Are you flirting with the detective? That isn't in the stage directions. The character is panicked, shocked maybe. Jack.

JACK: "Oh no, I can't believe it. I think he's dead!"

MIRIAM: Maybe a touch of expression needed.

HELENA: My turn. You can all follow my lead. "Oh no, I can't believe it. I think he's dead!"

MIRIAM: Very erm, very....

ADAM: Dramatic.

MIRIAM: Exactly. Very dramatic. Andrea, would you like to go?

ANDREA: Not really.

HELENA: Just do it. We all know the part will be mine, so it doesn't really matter how good or bad you are.

ANDREA: "Oh no, I can't believe..." I can't believe I'm doing this.

ADAM: Ditto.

MIRIAM: Mildred, step forward.

MILDRED: "Oh no, I can't believe it. I think he's dead!"

MIRIAM: Well, that wasn't lacking in expression was it? And last but not least; Lola.

FIONA: (*Mumbling*) It's Fiona.

(*They step towards her.*)

MIRIAM: What did you say love?

FIONA: (*Quietly.*) My name is Fiona.

MIRIAM: Of course it is, dear, now deliver the line.

FIONA: (*Whispers.*) "Oh no, I can't believe it I think he's dead."

MIRIAM: Okay, that's everyone.

HELENA: And the lead goes to…

MIRIAM: Okay that was…What was that Adam?

ADAM: Shite.

MIRIAM: Not my choice of word, but it does suitably encapsulate the moment. Let's try a different line. "It couldn't have been me; I was…" you can improvise the rest of the line.

JULIE: I love a bit of improv.

SUE: You would.

MIRIAM: Are we all ready?

(*Silence.*)

ADAM: You all need to try a bit harder.

MIRIAM: Can you start us off, Julie?

(*They all deliver slightly louder, but the quality doesn't change.*)

JULIE: Of course. "It couldn't have been me; I was out at the time meeting a mystery lover who is married to someone else."

SUE: Slut.

MIRIAM: Thank you, Julie. It's always brave to go first. Let's continue down the line.

MIA: "It couldn't have been me; I was with my husband having a scan, which was supposed to be a secret but he has no filter."

JULIE: Or morals (*She looks at **SUE**.*).

MIRIAM: How wonderful using a real-life situation to express yourself. Sue.

SUE: "It couldn't have been me; I wasn't there."

MIRIAM: Short and impacting. Your turn, Jennifer.

JEN: "It couldn't have been me; I was out with my boyfriend, he's very sexy and knows how to…"

JACK: Did she say she's got a boyfriend? More's the pity.

MIRIAM: Moving on. Jack, you go next.

JACK: I get a go with Jen next?

MIRIAM: No, Jack, you get to deliver the line next.

JACK: But I'm the stiff.

MILDRED: Fine, I'll go next. "It couldn't have been me; I was auditioning for a fabulous Shakespearean acting opportunity at the time, and yes I did get the part."

HELENA: Okay I think I'm next. I would just like to apologise in advance to anyone I inadvertently make feel inadequate. It is simply because I have more experience as per my substantial CV. Do you mind if I step forward, Miriam? I need to feel like I'm in the spotlight, it helps with focus.

MIRIAM: Absolutely.

HELENA: "It couldn't have been me; I was on set with Hugh Jackman."

SUE: Name dropper.

HELENA: "It couldn't have been me; I was on the set with Hugh Jackman. It was the final day of filming and we were approaching the kissing scene. I knew my chances of an Academy Award were high so I had to get the intimacy just right."

MIRIAM: Lovely, Helena.

SUE: Bullshit.

HELENA: I haven't finished. You didn't set a time limit. I have an entire monologue, which includes my Academy Award speech.

MIRIAM: You were fabulous; we don't need to hear more. Andrea is up next.

ANDREA: "It couldn't have been me; I was busy making props."

*(**ADAM** is getting gradually more intoxicated.)*

ADAM: For God's sake, Miriam, let her do props. This is a shit show as it is.

MIRIAM: I do not appreciate your tone. I have put my heart and soul into this.

MIA: I think you need to cut back on the whisky, love.

SUE: Love?

JULIE: What is your problem?

SUE: You're my problem, he's my problem.

JEN: Let's just calm down. Look; Fiona is trying to speak.

(Everyone steps forward.)

JULIE: Is she doing her improv?

ANDREA: Don't worry, Fiona. You can do props with me.

MIRIAM: No one else is on props. My play is minimalist, I need actors not objects.

Task:

Read through the extract and make a character profile of each role in this scene. Examine their character traits in as much detail as possible. In groups, create a back story for one of the characters and create a scene that gives the audience insight into their life before they joined the amateur dramatics group, staying true to their character traits.

Do any of the characters' stories interlink? Have they met before? Write or improvise a duologue between two of the characters. Is there a clear protagonist/antagonist?

Below is an example that explores Mildred and Adam meeting for the first time.

*(We see a flashback of **MILDRED's** first audition.)*

ADAM: Welcome to Ainsfield's ninth anniversary production of...

MILDRED: Where do you want me?

ADAM: And you are?

MILDRED: Mildred.

ADAM: Ah yes, Mildred, and you are auditioning for?

MILDRED: Witch One.

ADAM: Yes, that's what I'm asking you.

MILDRED: Witch One.

ADAM: Yes, which one are you auditioning for? Which is your role of preference in our ninth anniversary production of...?

MILDRED: I'm here to audition for Witch One.

ADAM: Witch One? Do you mean the Wicked Witch of the West?

MILDRED: No, I mean Witch One, should I start? Double, double toil and...

ADAM: That's Macbeth.

MILDRED: No, it's Witch One.

ADAM: Yes, Macbeth!

MILDRED: No, it's definitely by Shakespeare.

ADAM: Yes, William Shakespeare who wrote Macbeth.

MILDRED: Ah yes, then you're right. I'm here to be your Witch One from Macbeth by Mr William Shakespeare.

ADAM: That's nice, Mavis.

MILDRED: Mildred.

ADAM: That's nice, Mildred, but this is an audition for Ainsfield's Amateur Dramatic Society's ninth anniversary production of *The Wizard of Oz*.

MILDRED: Could you maybe do it in Shakespearean language?

ADAM: Erm no, Mavis...Mildred, I could not; I will do it as the playwright has written it.

MILDRED: Well that's not very creative is it?

ADAM: OK, Mildred if thou wouldst like to leaveth through the dooreth, I will get on with my MUSICAL which I can promise you has no connection to the works of Shakespeare. And will be AADS's ninth anniversary production, complete with a yellow brick road made of real bricks, flying monkeys that actually fly, and no Shakespearean witches.

*(**MILDRED** exits in a huff.)*

ADAM: Flaming thespians! Next!

Task:

Improvise each character's first day at Ainsfield's Amateur Dramatic Society.

Choose one of the characters and write three short monologues which gives the audience insight into their thoughts and feelings, these should be set in the past, present or future.

In this play, the characters have to find a way to save their theatre after one of the characters has 'borrowed' money from the funds, and found themselves in rent arrears.

Discuss who might have taken the funds and why, then create a scene around this. How do the characters react when they find out? Host a hot seating activity or chat show scenario where the other characters confront the culprit.

How do you think these characters would try to save the theatre? Do they succeed or fail? Create the final scene.

Evaluating Performance Work

1. List words which best describe your character.

2. Describe your character's posture and give a specific example of when your posture changed and why.

3. What facial expressions did you use? Give three specific examples and explain your decisions.

4. Proxemics refers to your positioning in relation to other characters and/or the audience. Write down three examples of proxemics in your performance, and justify your decisions.

5. Give three specific examples of gesture used in your performance, and justify your choices.

6. Write a sentence for each of the following, referring to your character.

   i. Tone of voice (intonation)

   ii. Diction

   iii. Dynamics

7. Write a paragraph to describe your character's class and status within the performance. Does your stage status ever change?

8. How would you describe the pace of your performance? Was there suitable use of pause and silence?

9. Write a sentence to explain the tension in your performance. Draw a tension graph.

10. At what point in your performance is a climax reached? What skills are used to show this?

11. Discuss your character's body language and movement throughout the performance. When do changes occur?

12. Write a paragraph which explains the strengths and weaknesses of your performance.

Other Books Available by Joanne Watkinson

The Ultimate Drama Pot Collection

"A great series of monologues, funny, sad and heart warming. Like a little sidekick in paperback form! Extremely reliable resources for all genres of monologue. The author has, thankfully, broadened the horizons for anyone looking for suitable and appropriate audition material. Students will be thrilled to perform these fun, new, fresh, quirky and up to date pieces." Dave King (Drama Teacher and

LAMDA Tutor)

A Striking Friendship

"This well written play is an excellent reminder, not only of the financial hardships experienced by families during the miner's strike, but also the unbearable strain put upon friendships. A great read and an ideal play for a variety of groups to perform." Amazon Customer

Who Needs Enemies

"This is my favourite play from this playwright. With a great twist at the end." Rosie Buckley (LAMDA Tutor)

The Drama Pot Books

"A wonderfully diverse collection of monologues. Such rich, interesting and inventive scenarios for young students to explore. I would certainly recommend this book to any drama or LAMDA teacher." Luke Stevenson (Drama Teacher)

"I've used The Drama Pot for my last few drama exams. The children really enjoy the monologues and we have received great results. Highly recommended." Jacky Rom (Author & Drama Teacher)

Intrusion

Intrusion is an ensemble play which explores the world of protagonist Susan Jameson, a young girl who suffers from Intrusive Thoughts which have plagued her life. The play explores mental health issues related to this, including anxiety and OCD, and tracks her progress from child to young adult.

The play is written with flexible casting in mind. The size of the cast and gender balance is left to the director. The play works best in a stylised format, with music and movement playing a significant role.

Fleeced

There has been some unusual activity in Nursery Rhyme Land and Bo Peep has lost her beloved sheep Baabra and Baartie under suspicious circumstances. The Duke of York is brought in to lead the case and the play takes us on a 'Who done it?' style journey which culminates in a surprising outcome. There are a number of suspects including traditional nursery rhyme favourites like Humpty Dumpty, Wee Willie Winkie and the Queen of Hearts. It is action packed, funny and heart-warming.

The play is full of vibrant characters which children will be familiar with and will love to play. It has a large cast but could also be performed with a small group of actors using multi role play. Aimed at 7-13 year olds, but could equally be successfully staged by older children and adults for a young audience.

It Started With a Kidnap

Ainsfield's Amateur Dramatics Society is about to lose its theatre, someone has spent all the rent. Is there a traitor amongst the group? Jack, the oldest member of the group comes up with a dastardly plan which involves a kidnap and a ransom note, but is this the way to save the venue? There are disagreements, laughs, plot twists and heart-warming moments to keep the audience entertained.